Creating Stunning Dashboards with QlikView

Bring real business insights to your company through effective and engaging dashboards in QlikView

Julián Villafuerte

[PACKT] enterprise
PUBLISHING

professional expertise distilled

BIRMINGHAM - MUMBAI

Creating Stunning Dashboards with QlikView

First published: October 2015

Production reference: 1141015

Published by Packt Publishing Ltd.
Livery Place
35 Livery Street
Birmingham B3 2PB, UK.

ISBN 978-1-78217-573-5

www.packtpub.com

Credits

Author
Julián Villafuerte

Reviewers
Hakan Hansson
Speros Kokenes
Mark O'Donovan
Karl Pover

Commissioning Editor
Veena Pagare

Acquisition Editor
Larissa Pinto

Content Development Editor
Priyanka Mehta

Technical Editor
Parag Topre

Copy Editor
Shruti Iyer

Project Coordinator
Izzat Contractor

Proofreader
Safis Editing

Indexer
Monica Ajmera Mehta

Production Coordinator
Nilesh R. Mohite

Cover Work
Nilesh R. Mohite

Foreword

I will start with a confession: there is a past version of me that would have questioned the very publishing of a tome devoted to creating dashboards (much less to creating stunning dashboards). Why would we need an entire book on something as trivial as "formatting"? This is the easy stuff… right?

Indeed, I thought of myself as a serious data guy (and a semiserious coder). I had no time for such trivialities as RGB minutiae, pixel-perfect layout, and style sheets; and admittedly, my deliverables looked lousy! I probably violated every design principle in "the book" and perhaps even invented a few new ones.

In retrospect I realize this, but at the time, I was all about the numbers and a beautiful, symmetric data model. That's what pure design meant to me! Alas, as gorgeous as a perfect entity-relationship diagram or dimensional model is, the reality is that no one in your business will care. Certainly no one in my business cared.

Julián Villafuerte's *Creating Stunning Dashboards with QlikView* brings the dashboard UI to the front and center, where it really belongs. I'm sure many hardcore developers would argue with me on this (and certainly my past self would!) but the display of information and the telling of the story is as important as the numbers. Julian tacitly acknowledges this fact and provides us with a wonderful guide to realize this goal.

His writing flows seamlessly from pragmatic to theoretical, from perfunctory to humorous. He pays homage and proper attribution to the likes of Few, Tufte, and Rosling in the early chapters but quickly takes us on his own adventure. The myriad of images, code snippets, tables, and step-by-step instructions make the content easy to follow and straightforward to implement.

In addition to his writing style, Julian's visual design style also emerges in the book. Although very clean and minimalistic, it never comes across as cold or stark; rather, it comes across as warm and inviting. He's able to remove the "noise" while still presenting dashboards that you want to look at. He uses splashes of color and saturation to great effect and even an assortment of special icons. If other authors have led you to believe that such glitzy visual devices were verboten, I urge you to think again after you've had a chance to look at how effective they are in Julian's work throughout his book.

Be it a QlikView newbie or seasoned developer, there is something for everyone in *Creating Stunning Dashboards with QlikView*. It will help you get more eyes on your dashboards and better tell the stories within your data. And for those of you who are "all about the numbers", I would humbly suggest that this is a must-read.

Enjoy.

Bill Lay

Founder and Principal, William Lay Group

Los Angeles, 2015

About the Author

Julián Villafuerte is a founding member of Evolcon Evolution Consulting, a Mexican firm that provides QlikView consulting services throughout the Americas. Since 2010, he has helped several companies define effective strategies for data management and business analysis. As a consultant, Julian has worked in application development, project management, presales, and training for many industries, including retail, manufacturing, and insurance.

He has a master's degree in information technology management and teaches at the Tecnológico de Monterrey in Mexico City. Recently, Julian started a blog called QlikFreak (`https://qlikfreak.wordpress.com/`), where he shares tips and tricks for data visualization, scripting, and best practices.

This book would not have been possible without the support and patience of Paulina Montes de Oca. Thanks for being by my side at every step of this journey (and sorry for all the trouble).

I would also like to thank my lifelong QlikView partners, José Ángel del Río, Carlos Reyes, and Jaime Aguilar, who have helped me more times than I care to remember. And thanks to my comrade, Oscar Goñi, whose keen eye helped me make the best out of this book.

I am also grateful to my friends Dante de Gante, Arturo Moreno, Paulina Novaro, Ilse Van Damme, and Raúl Pardo, who have given me their full support through these years.

But above everything else, I'd like to thank my mentor, Karl Pover, whose advice has helped me grow both personally and professionally. It's an honor to work with you. Thanks for all your help, I really appreciate it. But don't feel so great, you're not thaaaat important.

About the Reviewers

Hakan Hansson has worked as a QlikView developer and architect since 2007, when he was introduced to version 8. He has worked with the data management, integration, and design of QlikView applications in many different environments and in fields such as sales, logistics, and finance.

Currently, Hakan is working as a senior consultant at Climber (`http://climber.eu`), which is the largest Qlik partner in Europe with experts in seven countries. Their services range from developing brand new dashboards and knowledge transfer to maintenance and support.

Speros Kokenes is a data visualization practitioner with several years of experience in bringing visualization best practices to QlikView applications. He has received several awards from Qlik for his dashboard design and development work. Speros leads a design team at Axis Group, an information management consulting firm that is North America's largest focused Qlik development organization. He writes about data visualization at `http://blog.axisgroup.com`.

Karl Pover is a Qlik Luminary and president of Evolcon Evolution Consulting (`http://www.evolcon.com`), which provides QlikView consulting services throughout Mexico. Since 2006, he has been dedicated to providing QlikView presales, implementation, training, and expert services. Karl is the author of *Learning QlikView Data Visualization* and the soon to be published *Mastering QlikView Data Visualization*.

You can follow him on Twitter at `@karlpover` and read his blog at `http://www.poverconsulting.com`.

Mark O'Donovan is a QlikView developer and author based in London, England. He has over 20 years of experience in the IT industry and has been working on SQL Server Business Intelligence projects since 2008. Mark has been using QlikView since version 9.

He has had an interest in visualization since his student years; his master's degree thesis called *"Towards a methodology for visualizing quantum computing"* was presented as part of a EuroGraphics conference at Imperial College, London, in 1996.

Mark has been an active member of the Qlik Community since October 2011 and has been the author/publisher (TechStuffy Books) of the following books on Qlik and SQL:

- *Qlik Sense for Beginners*
- *Practical QlikView*
- *Practical QlikView 2 - Beyond Basic QlikView*
- *Practical Sql: Microsoft Sql Server T-SQL for Beginners*

Here are some useful links to his content:

- `http://techstuffy.tv` (YouTube — regular videos on QlikView, Qlik Sense, and SQL)
- `http://techstuffybooks.com` (Books on Amazon)
- `http://udemy.com/u/markodonovan` (Video training)
- `http://techstuffy.com` (Blog and free book samples)

www.PacktPub.com

Support files, eBooks, discount offers, and more

For support files and downloads related to your book, please visit www.PacktPub.com.

Did you know that Packt offers eBook versions of every book published, with PDF and ePub files available? You can upgrade to the eBook version at www.PacktPub.com and as a print book customer, you are entitled to a discount on the eBook copy. Get in touch with us at service@packtpub.com for more details.

At www.PacktPub.com, you can also read a collection of free technical articles, sign up for a range of free newsletters and receive exclusive discounts and offers on Packt books and eBooks.

https://www2.packtpub.com/books/subscription/packtlib

Do you need instant solutions to your IT questions? PacktLib is Packt's online digital book library. Here, you can search, access, and read Packt's entire library of books.

Why subscribe?

- Fully searchable across every book published by Packt
- Copy and paste, print, and bookmark content
- On demand and accessible via a web browser

Free access for Packt account holders

If you have an account with Packt at www.PacktPub.com, you can use this to access PacktLib today and view 9 entirely free books. Simply use your login credentials for immediate access.

Instant updates on new Packt books

Get notified! Find out when new books are published by following @PacktEnterprise on Twitter or the *Packt Enterprise* Facebook page.

To my family, Gato, Poe and Ogoga. Thanks for always being there for me.

Mee papash. Poogh. Oxxoe.

Table of Contents

Preface

QlikView is one of the most powerful analytical tools in the market. Based on an in memory associative model, it lets users freely navigate through the data, spot trends, and make better decisions. This platform is capable of integrating a wide range of data sources, such as ERP systems, data warehouses, or spreadsheets, into a single application in order to display dashboards with state-of-the-art visualizations.

Creating a dashboard is more than just packing a couple of charts and tables together. It is a complex endeavor that involves understanding the business, working with multiple data sources, and presenting the data in the most efficient and elegant ways to foster discoveries. The adequate management of these three elements—business needs, data models, and visualizations—is the key to a successful BI initiative.

The art of communicating effectively is not one that can be easily mastered. A good data visualization can help users understand the current performance of the company and see details that cannot be seen otherwise. It is a means of presenting, explaining, and interacting with the information. When a dashboard is created with well-chosen graphics, insights come naturally. Throughout this book, we will embark on a journey that will take us from theoretical to pragmatic, sharing tips, tricks, and best practices, all in the pursuit of stunning dashboards that derive in tangible value for the business.

What this book covers

Chapter 1, Know Your Battlefield, Devise Your Strategy, is the starting point of this journey, where we discuss what lies behind a QlikView initiative.

Chapter 2, All about Dashboard Design Best Practices, presents a useful compendium of tips that will help you create a truly stunning dashboard.

Chapter 3, First Things First – The Dashboard Structure, explains how to create the skeleton of an application, including the wireframe, filter pane, and overall dashboard's style.

Chapter 4, It's Not Only about Charts, shows how simple text objects and tables can be the protagonists in a QlikView document.

Chapter 5, Handling "The Classics", focuses on tips and tricks regarding basic visualizations: bar, line, and pie charts.

Chapter 6, Creating Complex Visualizations, brings out the big guns and presents several examples of intricate graphics in QlikView.

Chapter 7, Enhance Your QlikView Experience, helps you define a library of useful resources that will speed up all your developments.

Chapter 8, Before You Go, closes the publication by describing what to do before, during, and after the rollout.

What you need for this book

You will basically need a computer with QlikView Desktop, which you can download directly from Qlik's website (http://www.qlikview.com/download). If you want to make the most out of this book, don't forget to also download the additional materials so that you can follow along the exercises.

Who this book is for

This book is focused on QlikView developers with a basic knowledge of scripting and layouts who want to improve their designing skills and build effective, eye-catching dashboards that deliver tangible value to their business.

Conventions

In this book, you will find a number of text styles that distinguish between different kinds of information. Here are some examples of these styles and an explanation of their meaning.

Code words in text, database table names, folder names, filenames, file extensions, pathnames, dummy URLs, user input, and Twitter handles are shown as follows: "You can solve this issue by using the `RangeSum` function."

A block of code is set as follows:

```
sum({$<
Type = {'Online Sales'}, Category = {'Books'}
Year = {$(=year(today())-1)}>}
Sales)
```

New terms and **important words** are shown in bold. Words that you see on the screen, for example, in menus or dialog boxes, appear in the text like this: "If you are dealing with a few items, you can keep the legend and use **Values on Data Points** to be more specific."

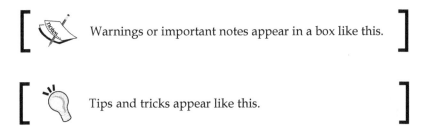

Warnings or important notes appear in a box like this.

Tips and tricks appear like this.

Reader feedback

Feedback from our readers is always welcome. Let us know what you think about this book—what you liked or disliked. Reader feedback is important for us as it helps us develop titles that you will really get the most out of.

To send us general feedback, simply e-mail feedback@packtpub.com, and mention the book's title in the subject of your message.

If there is a topic that you have expertise in and you are interested in either writing or contributing to a book, see our author guide at www.packtpub.com/authors.

Customer support

Now that you are the proud owner of a Packt book, we have a number of things to help you to get the most from your purchase.

Downloading the example code

You can download the example code files from your account at http://www.packtpub.com for all the Packt Publishing books you have purchased. If you purchased this book elsewhere, you can visit http://www.packtpub.com/support and register to have the files e-mailed directly to you.

Downloading the color images of this book

We also provide you with a PDF file that has color images of the screenshots/diagrams used in this book. The color images will help you better understand the changes in the output. You can download this file from http://www.packtpub.com/sites/default/files/downloads/8579EN_ColorImages.pdf.

Errata

Although we have taken every care to ensure the accuracy of our content, mistakes do happen. If you find a mistake in one of our books — maybe a mistake in the text or the code — we would be grateful if you could report this to us. By doing so, you can save other readers from frustration and help us improve subsequent versions of this book. If you find any errata, please report them by visiting http://www.packtpub.com/submit-errata, selecting your book, clicking on the **Errata Submission Form** link, and entering the details of your errata. Once your errata are verified, your submission will be accepted and the errata will be uploaded to our website or added to any list of existing errata under the Errata section of that title.

To view the previously submitted errata, go to https://www.packtpub.com/books/content/support and enter the name of the book in the search field. The required information will appear under the **Errata** section.

Piracy

Piracy of copyrighted material on the Internet is an ongoing problem across all media. At Packt, we take the protection of our copyright and licenses very seriously. If you come across any illegal copies of our works in any form on the Internet, please provide us with the location address or website name immediately so that we can pursue a remedy.

Please contact us at copyright@packtpub.com with a link to the suspected pirated material.

We appreciate your help in protecting our authors and our ability to bring you valuable content.

Questions

If you have a problem with any aspect of this book, you can contact us at questions@packtpub.com, and we will do our best to address the problem.

1
Know Your Battlefield, Devise Your Strategy

Long gone are the days when a couple of spreadsheets and simple charts were enough to analyze data and make discoveries. With a tidal wave of information coming from data warehouses, transactional databases, application logs, mobile devices, and social networks, companies urgently need better ways to process, organize, and consume the data in order to create tangible value.

However, how do you build dashboards that are not only robust but also engaging and easy to use? Chances are that you have already acquired an analytical tool to do so, and since you are reading this book, you have made a wise choice in selecting QlikView. However, a great tool does not guarantee your success in this endeavor.

Before we dive in and start creating bar charts and scatter plots, it is vital to understand the context around our applications. The true objective of a dashboard is to tell a story, to let the user explore the data, and ultimately to provide insights that lead to good business decisions.

Throughout this book, we are going to share some best practices, tips and tricks that will help you build outstanding dashboards that truly respond to your company's information needs. In this introductory chapter, we will discuss the following topics:

- The role of dashboards in your organization
- Defining your audience and their needs
- Handling business requirements
- Creating the perfect dashboard

Dashboards in perspective

Even though multiple authors have elegantly defined what a dashboard is, the industry still has an abstract—almost mystical—conception about them. One thing is certain: they are a means to display information. However, if they are well designed and adequately delivered, they can do much more than that.

It is vital to understand that a dashboard is more than just a couple of charts and tables packed together. It is a tool that helps users navigate freely through the data and shows them things that cannot be seen otherwise. They transform simple data into useful and elegant visualizations that help companies gain a better view of their performance and allow them to make better decisions.

Building a dashboard is not an easy task. It requires a great understanding of the business, a lot of creativity, and a robust set of technical skills. However, most of the time, the developers are so absorbed in the tools, calculations, and data sources that they forget the true nature of dashboards: supporting the business.

We will start our journey by defining some phases that will help you understand the business environment and devise a strategy that will ultimately lead you to creating a stunning dashboard. These are not intended to be strict norms that must be followed by heart. Instead, they should be seen as general recommendations that will guide your efforts in the right direction.

The six steps that will help you to start your dashboard initiative are:

1. Define your audience.
2. Spot the business need.
3. Choose the right KPIs.
4. Get to know your data sources.
5. Tell a story.
6. Enjoy the process.

Step 1 – define your audience

Dashboards are no longer tools that are designed exclusively for the CEOs who want to review the financial results of their companies. As more organizations realize the potential behind their data, the conception of dashboards as everyday tools to enhance operations, monitor business processes, and support decision making at all levels has substantially increased.

The first step to create a stunning QlikView dashboard does not have to do with charts or tables. Instead, your initial goal is to define who your audience will be. By knowing who is going to work with the applications beforehand, you can choose the best way to present the data according to their specific needs. So jump into your users' shoes and imagine what they would want to see in their dashboards every morning, what kind of questions they are going to ask, and which visual representations would be the best options to answer them.

For example, if you were working on a dashboard for the CEO of an international firm, you would probably have to avoid enormous tables that show even the tiniest detail of the operations. His strategic role usually calls for a broader view of the company, so this level of detail would only make him lose focus. A better approach would be showing the top metrics that define the company's performance and compare them to their objectives or even industry standards. On the other hand, if you were working on a dashboard for your company's help desk, it would be useful to have not only high-level metrics but also detailed information regarding specific issues and their resolutions. As you can see, picking the correct level of granularity early in the project can save you a lot of predicaments and help you choose the correct language for each audience.

Another example of this concept is the unit of measurement that you select to present the data. The same metrics can have different representations depending on the viewers' perspective and preferences. For instance, the CFO may be accustomed to seeing all the information in monetary terms, while the plant manager (in charge of manufacturing the products) is more comfortable talking about the gallons produced, pallets shipped, or watts consumed.

Building analytical applications is both a social and a technical endeavor. So, if you have the chance, take some time to talk to the users about their everyday needs and pains. After all, any QlikView application should be focused and built around them.

Step 2 – spot the business need

Now that you have identified your audience, you must assess what they are looking for. In this regard, most IT departments rely solely on a requirement-gathering document. However, this method tends to be not only boring but also quite ineffective. These documents are usually generic templates that cover every initiative regarding technology, whether it is about programming a Point of Sales system, creating a corporate website, or changing an email password; so, they typically fall short when it comes to understanding the rationale behind a new analytical dashboard.

To ensure success, you must go further and establish a conversation directly with the users. This dialog should focus on the type of dashboard they are looking for, but more importantly, it should clarify what they want to achieve by using it. By listening to them, you will get a better grasp of the current situation, understand their goals, and — hopefully — be able to provide them with a better solution.

Start by asking simple questions about the process or business unit in hand (sales, recruitment, call center, account receivable, and so on) and the difficulties that they face while executing and monitoring it. For example:

- What is the primary objective of the process?
- Who is involved? Are there third parties?
- Is there any specific problem you are facing nowadays?
- How do you evaluate its performance?
- Do you have a defined goal/budget/quota?

After that, ask them about the application they dream of. For instance:

- What KPIs do you want to see?
- Which filters do you need?
- Do you have any preferences regarding the visual representations?
- How often do you need to update the data?
- Do you have all the data sources needed to calculate those KPIs?

During this phase, it is also convenient to define the intent of the application. Whether it is to analyze data and foster discovery, present high-level KPIs, or just report operative metrics, each application should be designed differently depending on how it is going to be used. The number of tabs, the distribution of the filters, and the type of objects used to display the data are just a few examples of the elements that might change depending on the tone of the dashboard.

If you establish a true conversation with the users, these sessions could change a phrase such as *"we need a sales application"* to something much more descriptive, such as *"our biggest concern is to achieve this year's quota, so we must keep a close eye on the salespersons' monthly performance"*. In the end, a deeper understanding of the business needs will always translate into better dashboards and happier users. As you can imagine, the motivations behind a dashboard are quite diverse, but once you understand the true business need, you can act accordingly.

When I talk about this subject, I always remember a conversation I had years ago with the vice president of a financial firm here in Mexico. After reading an extensive requirement-gathering document that left me with more questions than answers, I went to his office to try to clarify the motivation behind the QlikView initiative. As the conversation went on, we reached a point when he defined exactly the application he needed in just a few words. He told me "Julian, I want a dashboard that lets me know who I have to yell at every morning. I will not be the one fixing the issues, so do not give much detail. I just need to know where the problem is and who is responsible for solving it". To be honest, the expectations he had of the dashboard had nothing to do with what the document depicted. Unfortunately, most of the time, you will find yourself in situations like this one, so I strongly recommend you to involve the business users as soon as you can.

 Steps 1 and 2 are not necessarily sequential. Actually, most of the time, they are carried out in parallel through workshops and one-on-one meetings.

Step 3 – choose the right KPIs

The term Key Performance Indicator (KPI) refers to the most relevant metrics that reflect the functioning of a company. They are calculated differently depending on the nature and goals of each organization. Whether you are working with classic indicators like the net profit, market share, and churn rate or new trends such as the number of followers and check-ins, there is no doubt that KPIs are at the heart of any meaningful dashboard.

Most of the time, the metrics you intend to show in your applications are already being captured and monitored. If this is the case, it is advisable to meet with the business unit that is doing it and ask them about the data sources, the frequency of reporting, the most common issues they face, and any other relevant information about the process.

A recurrent problem in big companies is that each department calculates the KPIs in different ways according to the data sources they have available and their particular interests (not always obtaining reliable figures). This could turn into an issue later, so it is better to address it early on by meeting with the appropriate stakeholders and selecting the correct data sources and calculations.

Metrics that matter

Choose only the most relevant metrics and avoid using KPIs that no one understands. If you think that there is a new KPI that should be included or an old one that should be taken out of the picture, communicate it to the stakeholders. Some companies often keep indicators more as a tradition than as something that adds real value to their analysis. On such occasions, an external point of view can help them fine-tune their ideas and envision a better dashboard.

There is a moment in a company's life when analyzing every chunk of data is important. However, having dozens of KPIs just because you have enough data to calculate them is not worth it. Just try to imagine the head of the HR department opening a dashboard in the morning and yelling, "Oh my God, the percentage of left-handed employees in our legal department is alarmingly high. We must take action!". This example may sound a bit extreme, but you get the idea.

In this regard, you must work side by side with the users to select only the metrics that really matter. There's nothing wrong with having a dashboard with only two or three KPIs as long as they are useful and have an impact on the business.

Step 4 – get to know your data sources

By this point, you should know exactly who your audience is and what they are looking for. Now, it is time to turn into the technical terrain and meet the raw materials you will be working with: the data sources.

Although data modeling is not the focus of this book, we cannot deny the fact that information and its adequate transformation are the foundations of any QlikView dashboard. Therefore, it is important to ensure that you have the appropriate resources available to fulfill the business needs described previously. In this regard, be sure to assess the following elements:

- **Type of data source**: Will you be working with transactional databases, enterprise data warehouses, Microsoft Excel files or application logs?
- **Connection**: Is the information in your premises or do you need to establish a connection to cloud services or other sources?
- **Ownership**: Is it an internal data source, or is it in charge of a third party? Is it governed by the IT department or another business unit?
- **Reliability**: Can you trust that the data is correct and complete? Is it likely to have quality issues?

- **Volume**: Are you dealing with a small data set or are you going to work with several millions of records?

- **Update frequency:** How often do you need to refresh the data? Do you really need a real-time application? Can your infrastructure handle it?

Having a basic understanding of these topics gives you a better perspective of the technical environment and may help you during the implementation of the dashboards.

Additionally, this phase is the perfect moment to bring out your inner data scientist and get your hands dirty. Don't settle for the charts and tables you have been asked for; give yourself the chance to explore the data. You might be surprised by the insights you can get from just playing with the numbers for a few minutes. Some interesting elements you can look at are:

- **Associations**: Load the data into QlikView and take advantage of the associative model by analyzing the relationships between the fields (green, white, and gray have never been so useful).

- **Cardinality**: Familiarize yourself with how many products, employees, and suppliers the company has. It can give you a better perspective so that you can choose the right charts for each scenario.

- **Rankings**: Is there an element that is consistently at the top of the lists? Who is the best salesperson? What is the best-selling product?

- **Distributions**: Discover the shape of the distributions of some metrics. Do all our stores have the same margin? Do we have certain territories where the employee turnover is higher?

- **Trends and fluctuations**: Time to create a calendar and check if we deal with a seasonal market or a random one. Are our stocks going up or down? What is their rate of change? Are they slow and steady or fast and volatile?

- **Correlation**: Is there a correlation between the customer's age and the average ticket? Or maybe between the types of materials we are using and the production scrap?

The more you know about the data, the better understanding of the company you will have. In consequence, your analyses will be significantly more robust and derive valuable discoveries for your firm.

Step 5 – tell a story

Building a dashboard is all about telling a story. The only problem is, most of the time, you do not know how that story will develop. It may become an epic fable of success, great sales, and operational efficiency, or it could turn into a haunting tragedy that depicts customer churn, high employee turnover, and quality issues. In either case, your dashboard should be able to handle it and communicate those insights to the users.

The best recipe is to keep it simple, focus on the key performance indicators, and start building around them. The idea is to create a robust and flexible structure that lets users navigate freely thought the data. As a result, our charts and tables will do all the work, and the story will smoothly unfold before their eyes.

In order to achieve this easy navigation schema, you just have to picture what the user will want to see next. For example, imagine that we are creating a sales dashboard for a worldwide retailer. We decide to start our story with a relevant indicator: the sales figure for this month. As we will discuss in the next chapter, numbers such as this have little value unless we put them in context, so we could opt to make a comparison against the budget or the performance for the same period of the last year, ending up with something similar to the following image:

Now, it is time to take out our Nostradamus cloak and try to foretell what *the next question* will be. After seeing an increase or a decline in the sales, a user could enquire whether she is dealing with a local phenomenon or whether it affects all the countries equally. In response, we could create a table with the regional performance, such as in the following image:

Sales Analysis: Worldwide Retailer Inc.   XL

Country	Sales 14	Sales 15	%		Budget	%	
	$2,296,273	**$2,241,811**	-2.4% ▼		**$2,211,719**	1.4%	
Mexico	$371,308	$373,277	0.5% ▲		$325,602	14.6%	
Switzerland	$352,669	$363,591	3.1% ▲		$361,182	0.7%	
France	$334,149	$349,445	4.6% ▲		$321,312	8.8%	
Brazil	$283,812	$279,880	-1.4% ▼		$331,265	-15.5%	
USA	$244,838	$248,000	1.3% ▲		$264,033	-6.1%	
Spain	$215,291	$221,384	2.8% ▲		$204,868	8.1%	
Sweden	$289,482	$213,422	-26.3% ▼		$267,213	-20.1%	
Argentina	$174,057	$192,814	10.8% ▲		$172,681	11.7%	

Once you realize that Sweden has had a rough year, you can turn the analysis towards each store or even take it to the product level; so our dashboard must be able to handle all these scenarios. As you can see, once you identify your audience and understand what objectives they pursue, it is easy to emulate their train of thought and build a dashboard that truly responds to their needs.

Step 6 – enjoy the process

Last but not least, enjoy the whole experience! For me, building dashboards is one of the most rewarding activities about being a consultant. It gives you the opportunity to interact with people from multiple functional areas and get involved with intricate business processes. Without a doubt, it is a great opportunity to learn in both the technical and the functional ends.

If somewhere along the way you feel discouraged, just remember that you might not be curing cancer or ending world hunger, but you are certainly supplying your colleagues with better weapons to fight their everyday battles. Building dashboards is a way for you to boost their abilities, help them work smarter, and hopefully, make their lives easier.

Moreover, if QlikView is a new tool for your corporation, you might be fostering a paradigm shift by moving their current decision-making process away from random hunches, preconceived bias, and #YOLO to a more formal, governed, and powerful information-based process.

Creating the perfect dashboard

A stunning dashboard is the sum of two things: a great data model and meaningful visualizations. If you lack any of those elements, the business impact that it could have will surely suffer.

QlikView offers a great variety of visual elements ranging from simple tables to mesmerizing gauges. However, the effectiveness of your applications will depend to a large degree on how well you apply them in each particular scenario. Remember that without the appropriate means to communicate, even the most robust model is nothing but a set of numbers. In the same manner, any visualization—as fascinating as it may be—will turn out to be worthless if it is based on incomplete or incorrect data.

Building a dashboard lies somewhere between an art and a science. If you want to succeed in this endeavor, you must take the best out of each world. From the art department, you must bring some creativity and innovation in order to make your application aesthetically appealing and encourage user engagement. From the scientific field, you must resort to disciplines such as computer science, mathematics, and statistics to produce meaningful representations that lead to insights.

Don't overdo it

Just as Quintilian used to say in the ancient Hispania, *the truly beautiful is never separated from the useful*. While creating a dashboard, you must strive to find the balance between engaging visualizations and effective analytics. Even though most of this book will give you tips on how to make aesthetic charts, do not be tempted to create objects just for beauty's sake.

Sadly, the idea that extravagant dashboards are always great dashboards is deeply rooted in several sectors. In part, it may be our own fault (speaking as a QlikView consultant), as many of the demos we build in the presales process tend to be a little more dazzling than they should be. In our defense, let us highlight that the purpose of those apps is to impress a potential customer and not to analyze data.

For some people, the number of gauges, animations, and overly complex visualizations is directly related to the quality of a tool. However, if an interface is packed with text, shapes, and colors, our brain will be forced to do some extra work in order to pick the important elements and put aside the noise. This will make it harder to interpret the information and ultimately diminish the effectiveness of the dashboard. As a general advice to beginners, try to focus on the functional aspect of your visualization first (the numbers are correct and the message is clear) and leave the embellishing for later.

Paradoxically, the experts tend to fall in this trap quite often as well. Yet, their reasons are totally different. Once you feel comfortable with QlikView's designing options, you tend to skip the conceptual part and jump right into the technical stuff (set analysis, visual tricks, overlapping objects, and so on). There is no doubt you *can* create certain charts, but take a minute to ponder if you really *should*. Never forget that if a dashboard fails to communicate in an efficient and effective manner, nobody is going to use it. As Benjamin Parker used to say, *with great power comes great responsibility*.

Embrace simplicity

Think about the battery icon in your computer for a while. It has an extremely simple design, yet it does its job perfectly. Though it may sound weird, a lot of its features are desirable for a QlikView application. Think about it: it conveys a clear message (how much energy is left), it uses an appropriate language (percentage and time), it looks elegant, and it even alerts you when you are approaching a critical point. Believe me, senior management would kill for a dashboard with those characteristics.

You do not have to look so hard to find simple and powerful visualizations. Take, for instance, your car's dashboard. The designers did a great job of selecting the correct KPIs and the appropriate means to display them (Well, most of the time… I have seen really awful cases). You have the time, speed, fuel, temperature, and even an alarm system that tells you when the brakes need attention, everything presented in just a glance.

Even though complex visualizations can be very powerful, you don't always need them to bring insights to the users. If you can convey a clear message using simple visualizations, such as bar or line charts, there's no need to overload the dashboard with intricate objects. However, be careful not to oversimplify. There is a huge difference between a simple and a simplistic dashboard. If you cut out more details than you should, you will end up with an empty application that lacks substance and will not be able to provide business value. The key to stunning dashboards is always balance.

Timely feedback

While creating a dashboard, the more feedback you get, the better the final version will be; so, do not hesitate to ask for opinions. The most successful QlikView applications that I have seen are the result of continuous improvements pointed out by other developers, project managers, and business users. A stunning application is rarely a one-man effort.

Of course, you know your team members better than anyone. You might recall certain users that would be more of a threat than an ally in early stages, but there are other colleagues that may prove helpful along the way. Some of them can help you improve your understanding of the internal processes, share their knowledge about business rules, or even help you with usability tests. In the end, it is up to you to decide who you are going to select for feedback and when to do it.

Regardless of the development methodology you are using, building a dashboard is—by its nature—an iterative process, so you might try several times before landing the perfect dashboard. In this regard, I strongly recommend you to not get married to your first ideas as they may be slightly modified—or completely taken out of the game—in the feedback sessions. Focus on the big picture and remember that ultimately, the result of this effort should be focused around the business needs and not on your personal preferences.

Summary

In this introductory chapter, we reviewed the role of QlikView applications in the organization and shared some tips on how to start your adventure of creating a new dashboard. The six steps portrayed in this section will help you focus on what is important by giving you a 360-degree view of the business context. If you apply them consistently, your understanding of the company will improve, and your applications will be more valuable.

In the next chapter, we will review how to apply the best practices from all-time design gurus such as Stephen Few, Edward Tufte, and Alberto Cairo in our applications. It is going to get really interesting, so read on!

2
All about Dashboard Design Best Practices

Data visualization is a field in constant evolution. However, some concepts have proven their value time and again throughout the years and have become what we call *best practices*. These notions should not be seen as strict rules that must be applied without any further consideration but as a series of tips that will help you create better applications.

If you are a beginner, try to stick to them as much as you can. They will save you a lot of trouble and greatly enhance your first endeavors. On the other hand, if you are an advanced developer, combine them with your personal experiences in order to build the ultimate dashboard.

Some guidelines in this chapter come from widely renowned characters in the field of data visualization, such as Stephen Few, Edward Tufte, John Tukey, Alberto Cairo, and Nathan Yau. If any of these concepts strikes your attention, I strongly recommend you to read more about it in their books. Throughout this chapter, we will discuss the following topics:

- Dashboard design best practices
- Data-ink ratio and chart junk
- Using white space, alignment, and distribution
- Selecting the appropriate chart type

Dashboard design best practices

Throughout this section, we will review some useful recommendations that will help you create not only engaging, but also effective and user-friendly dashboards. Remember that they may apply differently depending on the information displayed and the audience you are working with. Nevertheless, they are great guidelines in the field of data visualization, so do not hesitate to consider them in all your developments.

Gestalt principles

In the early 1900s, the Gestalt School of Psychology conducted a series of studies on human perception in order to understand how our brain interprets forms and recognizes patterns. Understanding these principles might help you create a better structure for your dashboard and make your charts easier to interpret.

- **Proximity**: When we see multiple elements located near one another, we tend to see them as a group. For example, we can visually distinguish clusters in a scatter plot by grouping the dots according to their position.

- **Similarity**: Our brain associates elements that are similar to each other (shape, size, color, or orientation). For example, consider a chart with color encoding. Even if they are not grouped, we can associate the bars that share the same color.

- **Enclosure**: If a border surrounds a series of objects, we perceive them as a group. For example, if a scatter plot has two reference lines that wrap the elements between 20 and 30 percent, we automatically see them as a cluster.

- **Closure**: When we detect a figure that looks incomplete, we tend to perceive it as a closed structure. For example, even if we discarded the borders of a bar chart, the axes would form a region that our brain isolates without the need of extra lines.

- **Continuity**: If a number of objects are aligned, we usually perceive them as a continuum. For instance, consider the notion of different blocks of code when you indent a QlikView script.

- **Connection**: If a set of objects are connected by a line, we also see them as a group. For example, a scatter plot with lines and symbols (dots connected by lines).

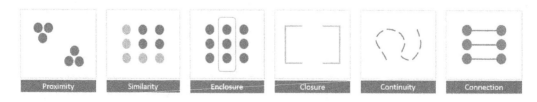

Giving context to the data

When it comes to analyzing data, context is everything. If you present isolated figures, users will have a hard time trying to find the story hidden behind them. For example, if I told you that the gross margin of our company was 16.5 percent during the first quarter of 2015, would you evaluate it as a positive or as a negative sign? It's pretty difficult, right? But, what if we added some extra information to complement this KPI?

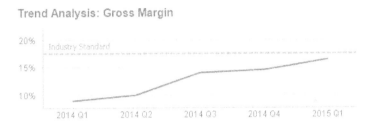

As you see in the preceding image, adding context to the data can make the landscape look quite different. Now, it is easy to notice that even though the gross margin has substantially improved during the last year, our company still has some work to do in order to be competitive and surpass the industry standard.

The appropriate references may change depending on the KPI you are dealing with and the goals of the organization, but some common examples are as follows:

- The last year's performance
- The quota/budget/objective
- Comparisons with the closest competitors/products/employees
- The market share
- Industry standards

Another good tip in this regard is to anticipate the comparisons. If you display the figures regarding the monthly quota and the actual sales, save the users some mental calculations and include complementary indicators, such as the gap between them and the percentage of completion.

Data-Ink Ratio

One of the most interesting principles in the field of data visualization is the Data-Ink Ratio, introduced by Edward R. Tufte in his book, *The Visual Display of Quantitative Information* (a must-read for every QlikView designer). In this publication, he states that there are two different types of ink (or in our case, pixels) in any chart:

- **Data-Ink**: This includes all the nonerasable portions of the graphic that are used to represent the actual data. These pixels are the core of the visualization and cannot be removed without losing some of its content.

- **Non-Data-Ink**: This includes any other elements that's not directly related to the data or that don't convey anything meaningful to the reader.

Based on these concepts, he defined Data-Ink Ratio as the proportion of a graphic's ink devoted to the nonredundant display of information. It can be represented as follows:

Data Ink Ratio = Data Ink / Total Ink

As you can imagine, our goal is to maximize this number by decreasing the non-data-ink used in our dashboards. For example, the chart to the left has a low data-ink ratio due to the usage of 3D effects, shadows, backgrounds, and multiple grid lines. On the contrary, the chart to the right presents a higher ratio as most of the pixels are data-related:

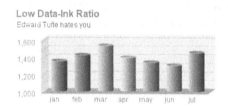

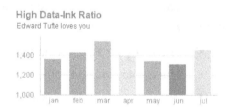

Avoiding chart junk

Chart junk is another term coined by Tufte that refers to all the elements that distract the viewer from the actual information in a graphic. Evidently, chart junk is considered non-data-ink and comprises features such as heavy gridlines, frames, redundant labels, ornamental axes, backgrounds, overly complex fonts, shadows, images, or other effects included only as decoration. Take for instance the following charts:

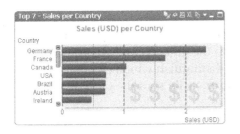

As you can see, removing all the unnecessary elements in a chart improves its readability and makes it look much more elegant.

Balance

Colors, icons, reference lines, and other visual cues can be very useful to help the users focus on the most important elements in a dashboard. However, misusing or overusing these features can be a real hazard; so, try to find the adequate balance for each one of them.

Excessive precision

As we mentioned in *Chapter 1, Know Your Battlefield, Devise Your Strategy*, QlikView applications should use the adequate language for each audience. While designing, consider whether precise figures will be useful or if they will only become a distraction. Most of the time, dashboards show high-level KPIs, so it may be more comfortable for certain users to see rounded numbers:

Revenue

$57,348, 229.82

▼ 2.632% vs Last Year

Revenue

$57.34 M

▼ 2.6% vs LY

3-D charts

One of Microsoft Excel's greatest wrongdoings is making everyone believe that 3-D charts are good for data analysis. For some reason, people seem to love them, but believe me, they are a real threat to business analysts. Despite their visual charm, these representations can easily hide parts of the information and convey wrong perceptions depending on their usage of colors, shadows, and axis inclination. I strongly recommend you to avoid them in any context.

Sorting

Whether you are working with a list box, a bar chart, or a straight table, sorting an object is always advisable as it adds context to the data. It can help you find the most commonly selected items in a list box, distinguish which element is bigger on a pie chart when the slices are similar, or easily spot the outliers in other graphic representations.

Alignment and distribution

Most of my colleagues argue that I am on the verge of an obsessive-compulsive disorder, but I cannot stand an application with unaligned objects. (Actually, I am still struggling with the fact that the paragraphs in this book are not justified, but anyway...).

The design toolbar offers useful options in this regard, so there is no excuse for not having a tidy dashboard. If you take care of the quadrature of all the charts and filters, your interface will display a clean and professional look that every user will appreciate. Take a look at the following images:

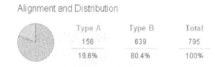
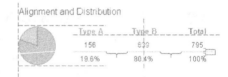

Animations

I have a rule of thumb regarding chart animation in QlikView: *If you are Hans Rosling, go ahead. If not, better think it twice.* Even though they can be very illustrative, most of the time, chart animations end up being a distraction rather than a tool that helps us visualize data; so, be conservative about their use.

For those of you who do not know him, Hans Rosling is a Swedish professor of International Health who works in Stockholm. However, he is best known for his amazing way of presenting data with Gapminder, a simple piece of software that allows him to animate a scatter plot. If you are a data enthusiast, you ought to watch his appearances in TED Talks.

Avoid scroll bars

Throughout his work, Stephen Few emphasizes that all the information in a dashboard must fit on a single screen. While I believe that there is no harm in splitting the data in multiple sheets, it is undeniable that scroll bars reduce the overall usability of an application. If the user has to continuously scroll right and left to read all the figures in a table, or if she must go up and down to see the filter panel, she will end up getting tired and eventually discard your dashboard.

Consistency

If you want to create an easy-to-navigate dashboard, you cannot forget about consistency. Locating standard objects (current selections box, search object, and filter panels) in the same area in every tab will help the users to easily find all the items they need. In addition, applying the same style, fonts, and color palettes throughout your charts will make your dashboard look more elegant and professional.

White space

The space between charts, tables, and filters is often referred to as white space and, even though you may not notice it, is a vital part of any dashboard. Displaying dozens of objects without letting them *breathe* makes your interface look cluttered, and therefore, it is harder to understand it. Some of the benefits of using white space adequately are:

- Improved readability
- Giving focus and emphasis to the important objects
- Guiding the users' eyes and creating a sense of hierarchy in the dashboard
- Fostering a balanced layout and making your interface look clear and more sophisticated

Applying makeup

Every now and then, you stumble upon delicate situations where some business users try their best to hide certain parts of the data. Whether it is about low sales or insane amounts of defective products, they often ask you to remove a few charts or avoid visual cues so that those numbers go unnoticed. Needless to say, dashboards are tools intended to inform and guide decisions, so avoid presenting visualizations that can be misleading.

Meaningless variety

As a designer, you will often hesitate to use the same chart type multiple times in your application fearing that users will get bored of it. Though this may be a haunting perception, if you present valuable data in the adequate formats, there is no need to add new chart types just for variety's sake. We want to keep users engaged with great analyses, not just with pretty graphics.

Choosing your weapon

Selecting the best chart types for your dashboard is a key aspect of QlikView design. With an ever-growing list of options flying around, we must focus on the message we are trying to convey and evaluate the pros and cons of each style. Although most of the time there isn't a single *correct answer*, I recommend you to base your decision on the type of analysis you intend to do and its required level of accuracy.

Level of accuracy

There is an outstanding study published in the eighties where William Cleveland and Robert McGill rank several methods for encoding data depending to how well our brain can interpret them. They point out that if a chart requires a lot of accuracy to be adequately understood, we should use the representations located in the left part of the scale (that is, position or length). On the other hand, if the visualization displays a general idea and doesn't require a lot of precision to be well interpreted, we can rely on techniques such as shading and color saturation (right part of the scale):

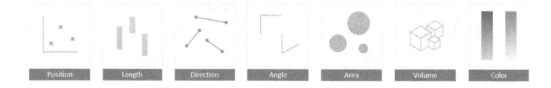

Based on this, if we want to compare the number of stores that our company has in each country, a bar chart would be among the most accurate representations as it uses the leftmost methods: position along a common scale and length. In second place, we can find area-based visualizations such as bubble charts (which are located in the middle of the scale). Finally, if we opted for a heat map (graphic based on color saturation), our visualization would convey the general idea, but it would be very hard to make precise comparisons between the items:

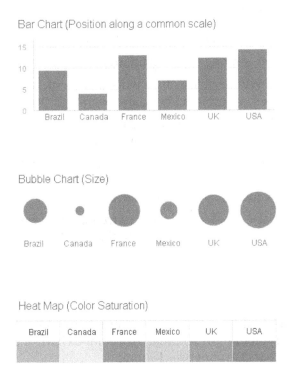

Types of analysis

The choice of the best graphic depends not only on the level of accuracy required to interpret it, but also on how well each chart gets along with the data and the type of analysis that it will support. Therefore, let's analyze the most common chart types and the scenarios where they excel or fall behind.

Bar charts

Created by William Playfair more than 200 years ago, bar charts are among the first and most popular visualizations. They are most commonly used to compare categories:

Here are a few points to note about bar charts:

- They are great for comparisons and rankings.

- Easy to interpret. Among the most accurate charts.

- They are amazingly flexible as they work great with multiple dimensions/ expressions, stacked/grouped bars, and even high/low cardinality.

- Be careful with the **Forced 0** option as it may change the interpretation of the data. We will learn more about this in *Chapter 5, Handling "The Classics"*.

- If the text in the axis is too long, change the orientation to horizontal. This improves the readability and lets you display the numbers at the end of each bar without the fear of overlapping labels.

- Bar charts can also be used to represent trends. However, instead of conveying an idea of continuity as with line charts, this style fosters a direct comparison between periods.

Dot plots

Dot plots are elegant—and often forgotten—alternatives for comparisons. They are built using only the **Symbol** representation in a combo chart. A dot plot has the same analytical power as a bar chart but uses less ink:

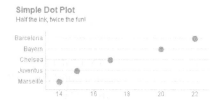

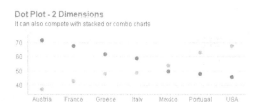

Dot plots are very useful for the following reasons:

- They are great for comparison and rankings.

- They are easy to interpret and very accurate.

- As they use less ink, dot plots are lighter than bar charts. If your interface is starting to look cluttered, they could be a better choice.

- Dot plots usually have a high Data-Ink ratio.

- You can use multiple dimensions/expressions by changing the color and type of symbol displayed displayed (dots, squares, diamonds, and so on).

- They can be very hard to read if you use too many dimensions/expressions, so don't overdo it. My recommendation is to use up to three data series.

Line charts

If you need to visualize a sequence of values representing a trend over time, your best bet is to use a line chart. It's simple, elegant, and meaningful:

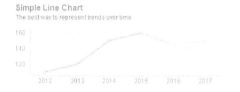 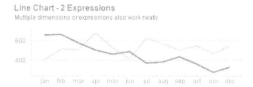

Here are a few advantages of line charts:

- They are widely used and easy to interpret.
- They can handle multiple dimensions or expressions (again, it's better to not overdo it).
- Vertical line charts usually don't work very well. Most people read these visualizations from left to right and understand this movement as the transition from past to present and, depending on the data, future as well. Therefore, unless there is a good reason not to do so, it is advisable to use the horizontal representation and apply the **Numeric Value: Ascending** mode to sort them.
- Adding symbols emphasizes the start of each period and can help the user spot the missing values.
- Besides changing the color of the lines, it is possible to change their width and style (continuous, dashed or dotted) to create visual cues.

Stacked area charts

Although very popular, stacked area charts should be used with extreme caution. These graphics can be misleading as they only use the axis as the starting point for the first component. After that, the new elements are placed one above the other; so, in order to interpret them correctly, you need to focus on the size of the layer and not on the shape of the top line.

Take for instance the following charts. If I asked you how our *green market* is doing, you will be tempted to read only the top part of the green area, pointing out a slight improvement. However, it is the size of the layer (highlighted with a red dotted line in the middle chart) that really matters. As you can see, a traditional line chart might be less appealing, but certainly clearer:

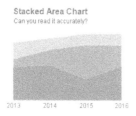
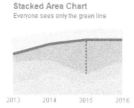
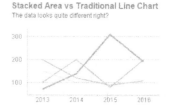

Combo charts

Combo charts are perfect for displaying multiple measurements at once. They can be used with categorical or time dimensions without any problem:

- Just like the bar, dot, and line charts, these representations are hard to read when you use more than three expressions.

- While creating combo charts, be careful with the contrast of the colors you choose. A symbol might land in a blank space or inside a bar, so your palette should be able to handle both cases:

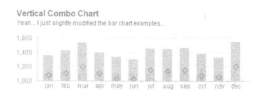

Slope charts

This kind of representation is based on a traditional line chart, and it specializes in showing a *before and after* comparison of two different points in time. Here are a few points about slope charts to keep in mind:

- Even though they don't provide much detail, they are a great way to spot the changes in ranking between two periods.

- If you are dealing with a few items, you can keep the legend and use **Values on Data Points** to be more specific.

- You can create an interesting visualization by keeping all the elements in gray and highlighting only the selected values. With this, you can focus on specific elements without losing the context provided by the rest of the data:

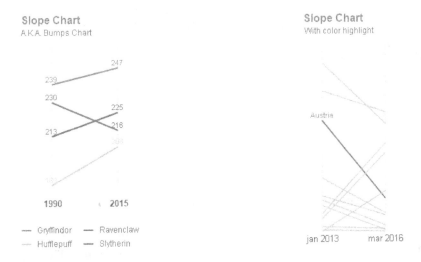

Radar charts

Seasonality is often represented using radar charts; however, they can be very difficult to read due to their circular axis. For instance, try to spot the month with the highest value by looking only at the graphic on the left-hand side. April, July, and October seem to be good candidates, right? Most of the time, a traditional line chart works better, so think twice before creating a radar:

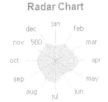

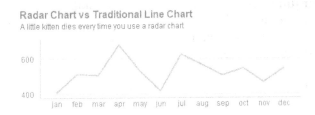

Pie charts

This is one of the most controversial charts in the field of data visualization. While it is true that our brain is not very good at reading areas and angles, pie charts are still the quintessential way to display parts of a whole (the word **quintessential** is brought to you by http://www.thesaurus.com/). In my opinion, most of the issues derived from this graphic come from misusing it and not because it is a bad tool per se. If you deploy them correctly, pie charts can be a great addition to your dashboards:

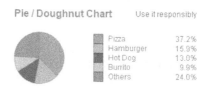

Here are a few points to be careful about while using pie charts:

- Pie charts are only suited to represent parts-to-whole relationships.
- I cannot emphasize this enough—never use 3-D pie charts. The angle and depth of the graphic can easily deceive the reader.
- If you have a pie chart with more than five or six slices, it might be a good idea to swap it for a bar chart or other visualizations.
- Sorting the values can help the user when two slices have similar sizes.

Other area charts

There are plenty of area-based visualizations—block charts, tree maps, waffle charts, or funnel charts, just to name a few. Sadly, they all suffer from the same problem: our brain's inability to compare areas accurately. However, when used in the right context, these visualizations can be quite handy, so don't delete them from your arsenal just yet:

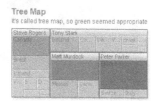

Stacked bar charts

We can also represent composition with stacked bar charts by adding new dimensions or expressions. However, this visualization might suffer from interpretation issues due to the offset of the bars. As we discussed in the previous section, length is not as reliable as the position in the Cleveland and McGill scale, so our perception may vary depending on the order of the bars:

 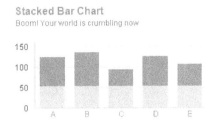

Scatter plots

Scatter plots are the best way to analyze the relationship between two variables (correlation). They can also help the users visualize several items at once in order to define clusters or spot outliers. It is a great option to explore a new dataset. Here are a few handy points about scatter plots:

- Scatter plots usually benefit from using gridlines in both axes.

- Though the simplest scatter plot is based on two metrics, you can display up to four measurements by changing the bubble size and color.

- Most of the time, scatter plots don't have a legend panel due to the amount of elements displayed. However, you can overcome this issue and let the user identify each bubble by adding a descriptive popup expression.

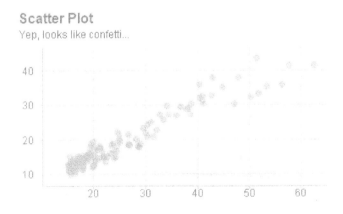

Tables

Even though they may be less appealing, tables are frequently the best way to present data. They can display a great amount of information in a small space and offer valuable features such as drag and drop columns, interactive sort, and pivoting. Besides, they can be further enhanced by adding visual cues, sparklines, and minicharts.

Tables are a key element to analyze data. A well-balanced application includes charts to promote insights and spot trends but complements them with detailed information via straight and pivot tables:

Tables							XL
Country ▾	Sales	Ranking	Cost	Margin	%	Trend	
	$1,112,982		**$943,187**	**$169,795**	**15.26%**		
Canada	$474,883		$390,866	$84,017	17.69%		
Brazil	$230,330		$198,849	$31,481	13.67%		
Denmark	$130,509		$114,516	$15,994	12.25%		
Austria	$114,869		$106,124	$8,744	7.61%		
Colombia	$101,632		$85,459	$16,172	15.91%		
Belgium	$35,288		$28,000	$7,288	20.65%		
Argentina	$25,471		$19,372	$6,099	23.94%		

Gauges and other forms of display for KPIs

Labels, gauges, thermometers, and bullet charts are great ways to highlight the key performance indicators. However, their overuse can be counterproductive, so limit their usage to the most relevant metrics only:

Reality	**52%**	Sales vs Quota		Sales:	$44,683,492
Expectation	61%		**55%**	Quota:	$81,766,949

Other representations

The chart types that we have reviewed so far are the most common visualizations used in QlikView dashboards. However, there are dozens of other representations that may be useful in specific situations, such as histograms, box plots, heat maps, trellis charts, sparklines, or geographical maps. We will review most of these in the following chapters, so stay tuned!

 If you want further guidance on choosing the right chart type, I recommend you to visit Dr. Andrew Abela's website, where he shares a practical flow chart to guide you through this process (http://extremepresentation.com/).

Summary

Throughout this chapter, we reviewed some of the best practices in the field of data visualization. By applying these simple tips, you can enhance your dashboards and transform them into truly engaging and functional analytical tools.

If you are interested in deepening your knowledge in this area, I strongly recommend you to read some authors such as Stephen Few, Edward Tufte, John Tukey, Nathan Yau, and Alberto Cairo. I assure you that you won't be disappointed.

In the next chapter, we will prepare the terrain for our charts by defining the overall dashboard's structure. We will talk about document styles, filters, backgrounds, and navigations schemas; so, turn on your computer. It is time to play.

3

First Things First – The Dashboard Structure

The wait is over, we know exactly what kind of dashboard we want, and it is time to start materializing it! So turn on your computer and open a new QlikView document as we are about to define the structure upon which our application will be based.

Though there is no formal categorization, we usually divide QlikView objects into two groups. First, we have the analytical objects. These are usually charts or tables, and their job is to present the right information in the appropriate formats. Secondly, we have all those elements that form the skeleton of the application and help the user navigate through the application, such as filters, buttons, current selections box, and other controls.

Although there isn't a correct order to create them (and most of the time, we find ourselves doing both at the same time), having the dashboard's structure built before you start creating the analytics often helps you overcome the blank page syndrome. With that in mind, throughout this chapter, we will talk about the following topics:

- Dashboard style and data distribution
- Filter panes and current selections objects
- Navigation schema

Dashboard style

Defining the dashboard style involves much more than just choosing a color palette and including a logo. While some developers consider it secondary, taking care of the look and feel of an application is imperative to turning data analysis into an engaging experience for the users. During the development, pay special attention to the document style, fonts, colors, backgrounds, and design resolution.

Document style

The **Styling Mode** is one of the first choices that you will face when creating a new document. By changing it, you can alter some visual features in the charts, such as the caption bar and the object's borders. In order to change this, navigate to **Settings | Document Properties | General**. Once there, you will find two options:

- **Simplified**: If you want a simple, good-looking, out-of-the-box style for your sheet objects, the **Simplified** mode is a good choice. It offers four different **Objects Styles** to work with:

 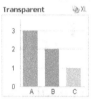

- **Advanced**: Activating this option enables extra features in the **Layout** tab of all the objects. Therefore, it is the preferred mode to create a customized look in your dashboards:

 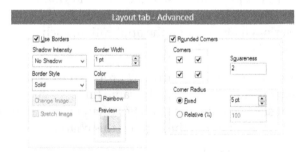

 If you go to **Settings | User Preferences | Design**, you can modify the default **Style Mode** and **Sheet Object Styles** options.

Fonts

Select legible fonts and use appropriate sizes to ensure readability. Believe me, no one enjoys working with dashboards built entirely using Comic Sans or Lucida Handwriting.

There are two main types of fonts: serif and sans serif (with and without serif). Serifs are the small lines tailing from the edges of the letters. They usually make individual symbols more distinctive, so our brain can process them faster as a result. However, the sans serif family is clearer at smaller sizes and displays higher readability on screens:

Times New Roman
Serif

Arial
Sans Serif

I shot the
serif

While we must strive for consistency, there is no harm in mixing different fonts in a single app. A good recipe is to apply serif styles, such as Times New Roman, in the titles and KPI displays while using sans serif fonts, such as Arial, for the rest of the objects.

 Warning: Some fonts don't get along very well with certain devices; ensure that you check for compatibility issues in the early stages of the development.

It is also advisable to create hierarchies by mixing upper and lower cases, different sizes, and colors. This will help you highlight the important figures and make it easier for the user to follow the flow of the dashboard:

45 New Leads	Stock this week In Store + In Transit £1,114 K	Total Customers ONLINE 1,420	STORE 2,592

Colors

Color is a double-edged sword. If you use it adequately, it can enhance your visualizations and boost the overall usability of a dashboard. If not, it may confuse the users and make them lose focus. If you are uncertain about how to apply color in your applications, follow these tips:

- Create a palette that matches your dashboard's profile. A good approach is to take the corporate colors and create combinations around them.

- There is no need to be an expert in color theory to create friendly and balanced palettes. You can find plenty of online resources that will help you in this endeavor:

  - **Color wheel simulators**: These sites let you choose a base color and build several schemas based on the color wheel. The recipes are easy to create and usually have great results. My personal advice is to use `http://paletton.com/` and `https://color.adobe.com/`.

| Color Wheel | Complementary | Analogous | Split Analogous | Triad | Tetrad |

  - **Design websites**: Forums such as `http://colorpalettes.net/` and `http://design-seeds.com/` share a great variety of palettes. You can look for a specific color, search by category, or simply browse the most popular combinations.

  - **Other tools**: Programs such as **Color Detector** let you retrieve the RGB code of any pixel on the screen. This is a must-have in any QlikView designer's arsenal.

- Be consistent across all sheets and objects. This will make your applications look much more professional.

- Using contrasting colors help you to highlight the most relevant items in a chart. On the other hand, applying too many colors in a single visualization makes it difficult to identify the important elements:

Color Contrast
It is easy to spot the important bubbles

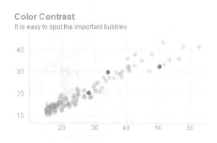

Color Galore
Using too many colors impedes focusing on the important items

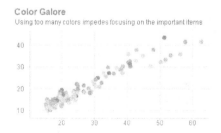

- While bright and intense colors are good to capture the user's attention, neutral colors are easier on the eye. If the users are to work with your apps for long periods, opaque or matte tones are preferred.

- There are three ways to *neutralize* a color:

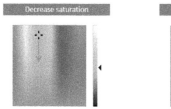

- Gray should be included in any palette as it helps to balance the intensity of other colors. Besides, it gets along pretty well with almost every style.

- Associate colors with ideas. For example, if you use blue to represent the sales in the first tab, follow that rule in the entire application. This will make your dashboards easier to follow and let the users work more efficiently.

- Respect the **RAG** convention — red for negative, amber for alert, and green for positive.

You can copy and paste any color tile by right-clicking on it. This is quite helpful to keep consistency between different parts (fonts, borders, caption bar, and so on).

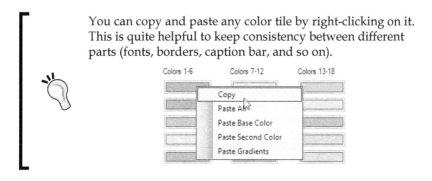

Backgrounds

A well-chosen background is a key element to build an engaging dashboard as it can improve its usability and create a more stylish look. When you create a new background, ensure that you take into account the following advice:

- Avoid using bright colors as they tend to be aggressive on the eyes and might end up stealing the user's attention.

- Keep a good level of contrast between the background and the charts to maintain the readability.

- It is acceptable to use logos in order to enforce the corporate image. As usual, try not to get carried away and include dozens of logos, labels, watermarks, and the company's mascot in every sheet.

- Use color strips, textures, and shadows to create subtle divisions that make it easier for the user to identify the filters, buttons, and analytical objects on the screen:

Logo   Time Filters

General Filters   Content

 There are a lot of useful resources to create backgrounds, such as strips, shadows, and panels in the **QlikView Developer Toolkit** available on **Qlik Community**.

Design resolution

Here's a piece of friendly advice—always define the appropriate design resolution before starting your development. If you don't consider it beforehand, you might end up restructuring the whole dashboard because it is either too big or too small.

Unfortunately, QlikView does not adjust the size of the objects to fit the screen (except for mobile clients), so you have to establish a standard resolution manually. Therefore, if your computer has a 1920 x 1080 screen, use visual cues to help you delimit the working area so that the applications look good at lower resolutions.

 QlikView apps are typically consumed in a web browser. As most of us use extra bars, such as **Favorites** or **Google Search**, it is a good idea to consider an extra space for them.

Layout and distribution

Well-designed applications always present the data in an ordered and logical manner. They usually follow a pattern that lets the user see the high-level KPIs first and then—as the situation demands it—presents a more detailed view of the data. A great reference in this regard is Qlik's **DAR** methodology, which divides the applications in three sections:

- **Dashboards**: High-level overview of the company or business process
- **Analysis**: Interactive tabs that let the user dig into the data by presenting a wider range of filters, charts, and tables
- **Reports**: Static views that present the most granular information

In the pursuit of a stunning dashboard, we should also focus on the distribution of the objects inside a particular sheet. The layout will depend on the type of analytical objects and the format of the filters that you choose to include. However, consistency and alignment should always prevail. Unlike other platforms, QlikView doesn't restrict the location of the objects to a rigid grid, so you can try countless distributions. Pick the one that best suits the information displayed:

For instance, the following application uses three main blocks—time filters (top), the general filter pane (left), and the analytical objects (right).

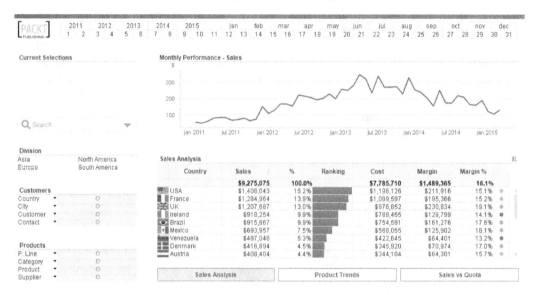

In contrast, the next dashboard changes the classic distribution and displays four blocks. From top to bottom: time filters, the general filter pane, the KPI belt, and the analytical objects.

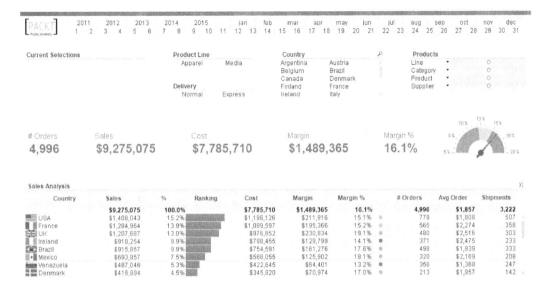

Country	Sales	%	Ranking	Cost	Margin	Margin %		# Orders	Avg Order	Shipments
	$9,275,075	100.0%		$7,785,710	$1,489,365	16.1%		4,996	$1,857	3,222
USA	$1,408,043	15.2%		$1,196,126	$211,916	15.1%		779	$1,808	507
France	$1,284,964	13.9%		$1,089,597	$195,366	15.2%		565	$2,274	358
UK	$1,207,687	13.0%		$976,852	$230,834	19.1%		480	$2,516	303
Ireland	$918,254	9.9%		$788,455	$129,799	14.1%		371	$2,475	233
Brazil	$915,867	9.9%		$754,591	$161,276	17.6%		498	$1,839	333
Mexico	$693,957	7.5%		$568,055	$125,902	18.1%		320	$2,169	208
Venezuela	$487,046	5.3%		$422,645	$64,401	13.2%		356	$1,368	247
Denmark	$416,894	4.5%		$345,920	$70,974	17.0%		213	$1,957	142

As you can see, there is no need for lines or other elements to enclose these blocks. The appropriate usage of white space and the Gestalt principle of proximity will do the trick.

 In order to keep consistency, try to limit the number of different layouts in your applications to three or less.

Also, when you are building a dashboard, think about it as a whole. While individual charts and tables can be efficient means to display information, when all the components of a sheet work together, insights and discoveries come naturally. Try to combine the analytical capabilities of the charts with the flexibility and detailed perspective of the tables. Remember that selecting an item in one graphic and seeing what happens in the rest of the objects is a valuable trait for business analysis.

Filter panes

As most dashboards require filters to refine the analyses or change the perspective of the data, it is advisable to include a robust filter pane to boost the usability of the application. After all, selections are the foundation of the associative model, which is one of the most powerful features that QlikView offers.

Only the most relevant fields should be taken into account for this purpose. Once again, it all revolves around your audience and their needs. While high-level dashboards usually require only two or three filters, detailed applications may require much more. In general, avoid including fields that do not add value to the business. Also, try to present them in a logical fashion:

- Group fields that belong together, such as a year, month, quarter, or weekday, in a specific area.

- Order the fields in a hierarchical manner. For instance, if you are creating a filter of the customers, it is a good idea to display the country in the first place, then include the city, and finally to add the customer's name.

Filter presentation

After selecting which fields to use, define how you are going to display them:

- **List box**: This is the most intuitive object; it is easy to read, easy to click on, and lets you appreciate the green-white-gray relationships. Only the most important or commonly used fields should be included in this format.

- **Multi box**: This is more compact but less intuitive (and also, a bit harder to use). This format should be used for elements that are not part of the main analyses but may come handy in specific situations.

- **Search object**: If you have too many filters but don't feel comfortable with a 25-field multi box, you can opt to include a search object that serves as a hub for all the users' selections. This is the less intuitive option because it doesn't show any value at all, so it is best suited for analysts who know the information very well.

- **Other types of filters**: Using a few tricks, other items can also serve as filters. For example, you can create a button that selects multiple fields at once or applies a bookmark.

The way in which you present the filters can contribute to creating a better navigation schema and offer a better user experience. Here are some practical tips in this regard:

- Use business-oriented names. Even though you can change the **Title** in a list box, it is advisable to change the names directly in the data model. In this way, the users won't get confused when they select the **Customer** field, but the current selections box displays **Cust_Desc_Short**.

- Some filters such as year, month, or currency are self-explanatory, so you can omit the caption bar and create cleaner interfaces.

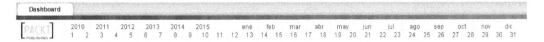

- Depending on the dashboard's layout, it may be beneficial to use list boxes with multiple columns. Just go to the **Presentation** tab and unselect the **Single Column** box.

- While displaying more than one column in a list box, you can locate the scroll bar either in the bottom or in the right side of the object (**Presentation | Order by Column**).

- If you want to save some space, create a container object that shelters multiple filters.

- Depending on the dynamic of the dashboard and the users' level of expertise, it can be beneficial to create drill-down or cyclic filters.

- In order to enrich the user experience and provide more context to the data, you can add expressions to a list box (numbers, gauges, or traffic lights):

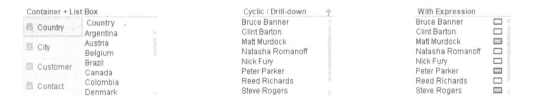

- If the information and the dashboard's style allow it, you can even create image-based filters (**Presentation | Representation | Image**).

- When using multi boxes, restrict the maximum number of items displayed in the drop-down list by going to the **Presentation** tab and selecting **Limit Dropdown** to **X Lines**.

Hidden Filter Pane

Another option to manage selections is to create a filter pane that you can turn on and off as needed. In this way, you can better exploit the screen space without limiting your users' capacity to select specific elements:

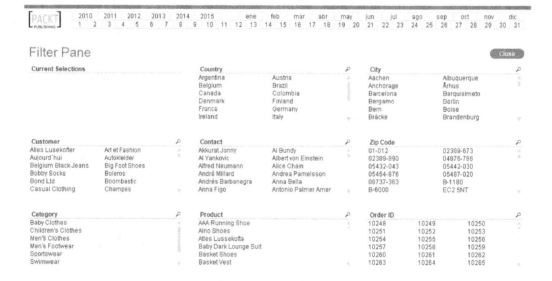

You can follow along this exercise by downloading this chapter's material from `https://qlikfreak.wordpress.com/books/`. Follow these steps:

1. Create a container object to shelter all the filters. Go to the **Presentation** tab and select **Grid** in the **Container Type** field. Also, increase the **Spacing** parameter to 10 points. This will be the white area that surrounds each box, so it is better to be generous.

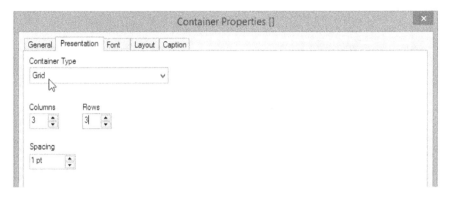

2. Drag and drop inside the container all the objects that you want to display. A current selections box accompanied by a series of list and multi boxes will work well.

3. Create a variable called `vFilterPane` (either in the script or by going to **Settings | Variable Overview | Add**).

4. Create a button (or a text object) that changes `vFilterPane` from 0 to 1 and vice versa by adding a **Set Variable** action.

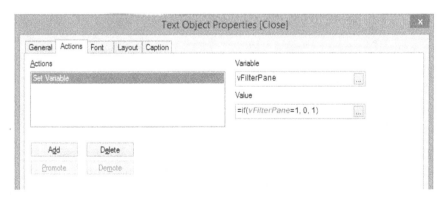

5.   We want this button to adapt its color and label depending on the content of the variable (whether the filter pane is on or off), so let's define a dynamic **Text** in the **General** tab.

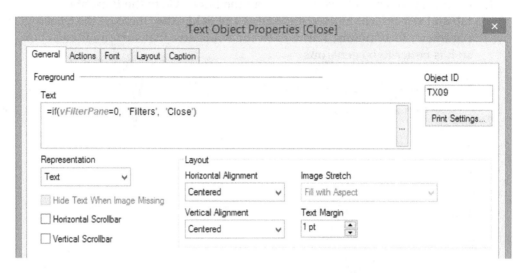

6.   Also, change the button's color by using this formula:

```
=if(vFilterPane=0, RGB(50, 100, 140), RGB(125, 125, 125))
```

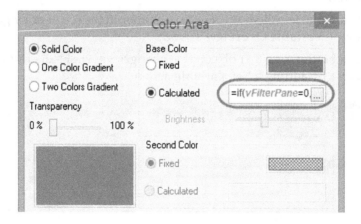

7.   Go to the container's **Layout** tab and tie its visibility to our variable by typing `vFilterPane` in the **Conditional** field. As the contents of this variable are either `0` or `1` (a Boolean value), there is no need to add any other logical condition.

8. In the same tab, choose the **Custom Layer** option and locate the container on top of the rest of the objects (higher layers cover lower layers).

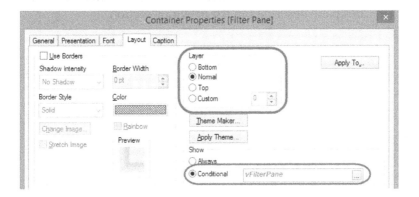

9. Done! We have built a filter pane that will be activated only when needed!

Current selections

So far, we have stated that all best practices are references that should be taken with a grain of salt. Well, this one is not: you should always let the user clearly see the current selections. QlikView dashboards tend to be very interactive due to the associative model. If your users lose visibility of which filters are applied, they can get wrong impressions and the decisions derived from them will be skewed. There are multiple ways to let the users know which selections are currently applied:

*   **Current selection box**: The most common and practical way to visualize selections is to add a current selection box. Although it takes some space, it is a great method to manage the filters due to the **Clear** and **Dropdown Select** options.

*   **All the filters are visible**: If your dashboard has few filters (and they are all visible), you can afford to omit the current selection box. Just beware of the selections made in other tabs as they may go unnoticed while returning to the dashboard.

 If you want to ensure that no other filter but the ones that are visible in your tab are active, just add a **Clear All** trigger when you activate the sheet.

- **Current selection footer**: A text object at the bottom of the screen is an elegant way to display the current selections while saving some space. In order to keep a good level of functionality, you can mix this solution with a hidden filter pane described in the previous section.

Trending Revenue over time

Revenue and Expenses

Region	Revenue	Expenses	% of Sales
Americas	$5,602,362	$3,555,748	63%
Asia	$3,923,164	$2,489,810	63%
Pacific	$1,072,894	$680,929	63%
Europe	$668,066	$423,987	63%
Africa	$99,565	$63,191	63%
Middle East	$18,978	$12,044	63%

Current Selections > Year: 2015 | Month: Apr | Category: Food & Drinks

In order to build this footer, you only need to create a text object that uses the GetCurrentSelections function. For example:

```
=if(len(GetCurrentSelections())=0, 'No Selections
Applied',
' Current Selections > ' & GetCurrentSelections(
'  |  ',        // Record Separator
': ',           // Tag Separator
', ',           // Value Separator
1)              // Max number of values
)
```

General navigation

As a QlikView designer, it is your task to organize data in a way that lets the users navigate comfortably through it and create structures that allow them to easily find what they are looking for. In a way, a good navigation schema is like your Internet connection. If it works well, nobody notices. If not, be prepared for a tidal wave of complaints.

Tab row

Just as books are structured in chapters, QlikView applications are divided into tabs in order to organize the information. Most of the time, you can rely on the standard tab row to do this job. However, if you need some extra spice in your interface, you can manage the sheets manually via buttons and actions. Just go to **Settings | Document Properties | General** and select the **Hide Tabrow** option. This feature is usually a little harder to maintain, but it can help you create a more stylish look:

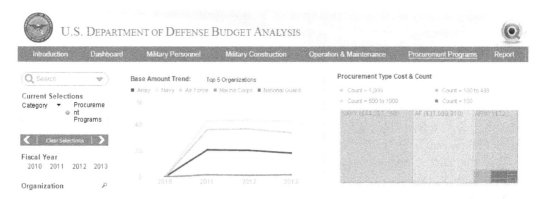

Showing and hiding objects

Our goal as dashboard designers is to build a robust structure that gives the users easy access to all the information they need. Most of the time, when you work on the navigation schema of a new application, it is necessary to create controls that show or hide certain objects depending on the flow of the current analysis. You can accomplish this in several ways:

- **Auto-minimize**: If your design involves mostly static objects and you only to need to switch between a set of graphics, the simplest solution is to use the Auto-Minimize feature (**Caption** tab). This option is easy to implement because you can adapt the resulting menu to the size and orientation that your dashboard demands. Just be careful with the alignment and distribution of both the minimized buttons and the expanded charts.

- **Containers**: The second option is to use a container object to shelter multiple charts. It is easier to maintain as it automatically adjusts the menu to the number of objects inside it. However, it is also a little less flexible due to its limited number of styles.

- **Object visibility**: The most flexible option is to modify each chart's visibility by adding a **Show Conditional** statement in the **Layout** tab. Although it might require some extra work, this alternative allows you to show or hide any object based on a selection, the content of a variable, or the user's credentials.

Logos

Traditionally, logos are classified as ornamental elements that only serve for branding purposes. However, you can improve your dashboard's usability if you endow the logos with some functionality.

What happens when you click on the logo of your favorite website? Most of the time, it takes you back to the home page where you can start browsing again, right? Well, in the same manner we can add some actions to the logos in our dashboard in order to return to its *default state*. This concept may vary from sheet to sheet, but it usually starts with a **Clear All** action, and after that, it may select the current date, the end of the previous month, or even a group of the most important customers.

By doing this, you will give the users an alternative to the **Clear** button that can save them a couple of clicks while making their QlikView experience more comfortable. Don't forget that a truly stunning dashboard is always created by paying the most attention to the tiniest details.

Summary

In the last pages, we reviewed some tips to create a useful base structure for our applications. Do not underestimate the worth of an engaging visual style, a well-designed filter pane, or a robust navigation schema, for these elements are the foundation of a killer dashboard. In the next chapter, we will learn how to take advantage of nongraphical elements such as tables and text objects to elegantly display information. Remember that, when building a dashboard, it's not only about charts.

4

It's Not Only about Charts

A picture is worth a thousand words; there is no way we can deny that. However, when it comes to dashboards, there is much more than only charts. Labels, images, and tables play an important role in communicating and understanding information. Besides, they can be a surprisingly effective and elegant way to display data. Throughout this chapter, we will review the following topics:

- Labels and images
- Straight and pivot tables
- Visual cues

Text objects

The simplest elements are often the most effective ones and text objects are certainly not an exception. You can include them in your applications in several ways:

- **Cover pages**: They give an overview of the application and often serve as a thumbnail in the Access Point
- **Images**: Frequently used for aesthetic and branding purposes
- **Titles**: Labels that describe the content of the tabs or groups of objects
- **KPI display**: This is a simple and effective way of presenting the main figures
- **Auxiliary labels**: Present relevant data, such as the units of measurement or the date of the last reload
- **Icons**: If well used, they can reinforce concepts or even substitute labels
- **Shadows and frames**: Visual elements that can help you create chunks of information or divide the screen into multiple sections

- **Traffic lights**: Visual cues that evaluate the performance of the company
- **Popups**: Labels that appear on certain conditions to guide the users through the application and remind them of the mandatory selections
- **Buttons**: Objects that help the user change tabs, modify variables, show hidden objects, and do much more

For heaven's sake, text object, is there anything that you cannot do?

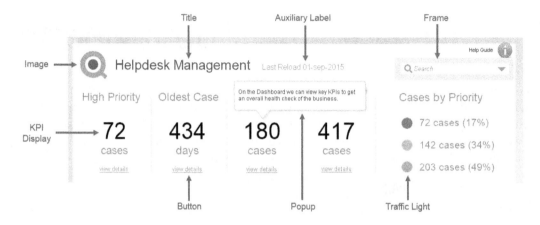

More than simple labels

In this section, we will share a couple of ideas that might help you enhance your dashboards using text objects in many different ways.

Displaying KPIs

An effective and visually engaging way of presenting the main figures in a dashboard is to build a *KPI belt* by combining text, visual cues, and icons. This type of visualization is very flexible as you can build the structure in a horizontal or vertical manner, use the fonts and colors that best match your dashboard's style, and present virtually any kind of information (raw figures, ratios, comparisons, and so on).

While it may look simple, creating these visualizations usually demands a keen eye, a lot of creativity, and a considerable amount of time. Nevertheless, once you focus on the data and find the best way to present it, the results tend to be stunning.

Here are a few examples of how you can combine objects to create appealing KPI displays. As you can see, some of them are as simple as a label with a modest caption bar, while others involve mixing fonts, colors, sizes, and icons to represent an idea.

Don't hesitate to create your own designs from the scratch. QlikView is a very flexible tool and lets you create amazing visualizations with just a couple of clicks. Just as in a Bob Ross painting, when creating a dashboard, there are no mistakes, just happy accidents. (Don't get too carried away; several happy accidents in a row might upset your stakeholders… especially project managers.)

Creating hierarchies

When we look at a dashboard, our brain automatically creates a hierarchy based on the position, color, and size of the objects that it displays. This is a preattentive behavior that allows us to pay more attention to the items that are considered more important. Therefore, you should be careful while formatting each component in order to highlight only the elements that deserve it. If you want to display a KPI, don't be afraid to use big fonts and bright colors. On the other hand, if you are building an auxiliary label, such as a timestamp of the last reload or clarification notes, it is advisable to deemphasize it using smaller fonts and lighter colors.

Selection prerequisites

We often deal with dashboards that need specific conditions to be met in order to work appropriately. For example, you might need to select only one year, have at least two products available for comparison, or assign a positive integer to a variable.

As you know, every object has a **Calculation Condition** that blocks it unless all the conditions are met. However, seeing a sheet full of error messages is not a pleasant view. Instead, you can create a text object that covers the rest of the interface and lets the user know which actions are required to go on:

In order to achieve this, go to the **Layout** tab of the *error* object (that is, the one that should cover the rest until the conditions are met) and modify its **Layer** to ensure that it is on top of everything else (the higher layers will cover the lower ones). After that, select **Show | Conditional** and add a formula to define when it should be displayed:

 Using semitransparent backgrounds (**General | Transparency**) usually works well in this scenario.

Controlling variables

Text objects are one of the few elements in QlikView that have access to the **Actions** tab, which opens a wide range of options for the designers. This feature lets you create more appealing buttons to make selections, activate sheets, create bookmarks, or even execute macros. Knowing this, you can use a text object not only to display, but also to modify the contents of a variable. Mixing these elements can help you create interactive controls that enhance the navigation schema and add new functionalities to your dashboards. Also, it is a great alternative to sliders and input boxes.

Transparent buttons

This is a dirty trick, so use it with caution. If you create a transparent button and set it over other objects, you can create the illusion in interactivity in elements that naturally don't have it. For example, the following dashboard displays six boxes with the main metrics for each department in a company. However, all these labels and images are covered by transparent buttons. When the user clicks on them, an action is triggered, and she is sent to another tab with specific information regarding that area.

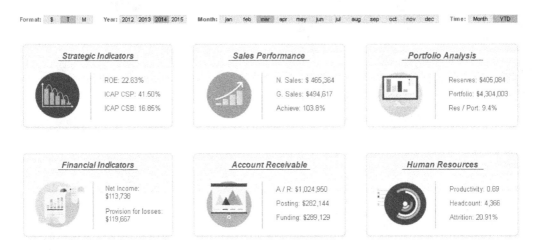

 If you lose a transparent item, activate **Design Grid** (*Ctrl + G*), and select all the objects in the sheet (*Ctrl + A*). After this, you will surely see the frame of the elusive ruffian and be able to put it back to its place.

Creating switches

The relationship between buttons and variables can go both ways; you can create a text object that modifies the content of the variable, which—in return—changes some of its features (background image, labels, colors, and so on). The best example for this behavior is an interactive switch button:

You can do the following to create this feature:

1. Create a new variable (either in the script or the **Variable Overview** window) called vMenu. This variable will control the switch.

2. Create a text object. Go to the **General** tab and select **Image** under the **Representation** dropdown.

3. Type the following formula in the **Text** box. It references two pictures depending on the content of a variable:

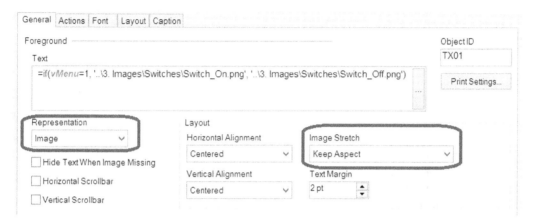

4. Go to the **Actions** tab and click on **Add**.

5. Add a **Set Variable** action (**External Action Type**) and introduce the following parameters:

6. Now, every time you click on this object, vMenu will change from 1 to 0 and vice versa. As a consequence, the switch image will also adapt and make its usage more intuitive.

It is up to you to decide what the impact of pressing this button will be. For example, you can link it to the expressions in a chart so the user can choose which one to see:

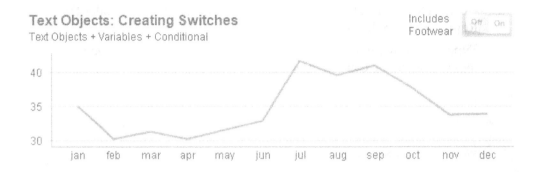

Interactive KPI display

Time to mix and match! We've discussed how to create a KPI display and how to build an interactive button. So, why not combine them? For example, the following visualization uses the three boxes on the right not only to show the variance in **Sales**, **Customers**, and **Budget**, but also to control the data that is shown in the table:

Sales Performance: July 2015 vs July 2014

	2015	2014		2015	2014	%		2015 Ac.	2014 Ac.	%	
				$276,940,087	$244,224,883	13.4% ▲		$276,940,087	$244,224,883		
mié	01-jul	01-jul	mar	$7,991,163	$6,778,904	17.9% ▲		$7,991,163	$6,778,904	17.9% ▲	
jue	02-jul	02-jul	mié	$8,188,736	$6,935,442	18.1% ▲		$16,179,899	$13,714,346	18.0% ▲	
vie	03-jul	03-jul	jue	$9,470,399	$7,046,171	34.4% ▲		$25,650,298	$20,760,517	23.6% ▲	
sáb	04-jul	04-jul	vie	$11,084,685	$8,770,553	26.4% ▲		$36,734,983	$29,314,070	24.4% ▲	
dom	05-jul	05-jul	sáb	$12,603,917	$9,783,099	28.9% ▲		$49,338,899	$39,314,169	25.5% ▲	
lun	06-jul	06-jul	dom	$7,036,259	$11,356,340	-38.0% ▼		$56,375,159	$50,670,509	11.3% ▲	
mar	07-jul	07-jul	lun	$7,397,223	$6,239,133	18.6% ▲		$63,772,382	$56,909,642	12.1% ▲	
mié	08-jul	08-jul	mar	$7,732,396	$6,260,035	23.5% ▲		$71,504,778	$63,169,677	13.2% ▲	
jue	09-jul	09-jul	mié	$7,924,355	$6,738,087	17.6% ▲		$79,429,133	$69,907,764	13.6% ▲	
vie	10-jul	10-jul	jue	$9,844,250	$7,390,923	33.2% ▲		$89,273,383	$77,298,686	15.5% ▲	
sáb	11-jul	11-jul	vie	$10,497,699	$8,927,428	17.6% ▲		$99,771,081	$86,226,114	15.7% ▲	
dom	12-jul	12-jul	sáb	$12,012,419	$9,509,372	26.3% ▲		$111,783,500	$95,735,486	16.8% ▲	
lun	13-jul	13-jul	dom	$7,930,272	$9,526,903	-16.8% ▼		$119,713,772	$105,262,389	13.7% ▲	
mar	14-jul	14-jul	lun	$10,234,485	$7,260,628	41.0% ▲		$129,948,257	$112,523,017	15.5% ▲	
mié	15-jul	15-jul	mar	$8,454,428	$9,301,346	-9.1% ▼		$138,402,684	$121,824,363	13.6% ▲	
jue	16-jul	18-jul	mié	$8,613,395	$7,656,537	12.5% ▲		$147,016,080	$129,480,900	13.5% ▲	

Sales
+ 13.4%

Customers
+ 5.8%

vs Budget
- 0.5%

The magic behind this lies in a variable that shows or hides the tables to the left while also modifying the buttons' backgrounds. The former is achieved by restricting each chart's visibility (just as we did in the *Selection prerequisites* section) and the latter is done by calculating the color instead of using a fixed one. For instance, refer to the following code:

```
if(vMenu='Sales', RGB(245, 245, 245), white())
```

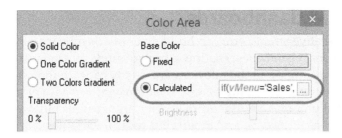

Unconventional visualizations

Text objects excel at displaying the main figures in a dashboard, mostly due to their flexibility. You can use them to change the size, font, color, and transparency of a label or simply to add an image. This allows you to represent data in innovative ways. Take for instance the following image:

This is a visualization that depicts the first part of a procurement process. The icons represent each step that must be fulfilled in order to make a purchase. The numbers on top of the arrows represent the average number of days taken to finish the task, and the ones at the bottom illustrate the percentage of the submissions that survive. For example, once they have a quotation, this company spends 7.6 days on average to get the approval from the corresponding managers. Also, only 85 percent of the requests make it through (thus, 15 percent get rejected).

Even though you could display the same information in a traditional table, using this kind of representations often makes the interface easier to understand and gives the user a more pleasant experience.

Handcrafted dashboards

If you are on a creative streak, you can build an entire dashboard using mostly text objects: labels, icons, visual cues, shadows, backgrounds, buttons, and so on. Such interfaces look amazing on mobile devices and easily capture the user's attention. However, do not forget that complex visualizations require a lot of maintenance; every change that you make will require moving transparent buttons, adjusting the alignment of dozens of objects, and modifying several variables.

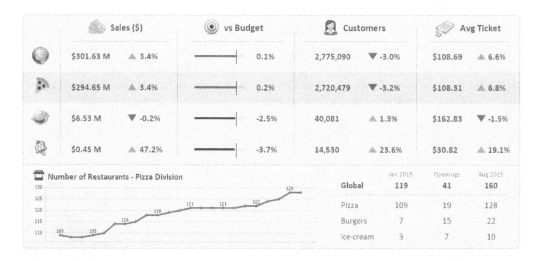

Tables

Tables are a simple, yet very powerful, means for visualizing data. Despite the fact that some designers disregard them due to their lack of visual impact, these objects are an integral part of any robust application in QlikView. Most of the time, charts are the preferred medium to spot trends and find outliers, but a table's ability to show great amounts of data in a flexible and accurate manner makes it an invaluable element for dashboard designers.

QlikView offers three options to display information in a tabular format:

- **Straight table (chart object)**: This is one of the most flexible objects in QlikView. You can include as many dimensions and expressions as you want (just be careful with the horizontal scroll bar). It has two awesome features that boost its usability: column drag and drop and the ability to dynamically sort the data depending on the user's needs (**Interactive Sort**).

- **Pivot table (chart object)**: If you need to distribute data among multiple dimensions and see the subtotals for each group, the pivot table is your best choice. Though less flexible than straight tables, they offer a unique feature — the ability to create **cross tables**.

- **Table box:** This object is rarely seen in finished dashboards. However, it is a great tool for developers as it shows the associations between multiple fields and all their possible combinations.

Spicing up tables

Having a detailed view of the information is reason enough to include tables in your applications. However, you can further enhance these visualizations by adding extra features that help draw the user's attention to the most relevant lines.

Adding colors

The easiest way to add context to a table is to change the colors of certain columns or rows. These changes usually respond to one of the following rationales:

- **Usability/aesthetics**: If you change the background color of specific elements, you can create chunks of data that are easier to interpret. For instance, the colors that divide the hierarchy of a financial statement can be set as follows:

Income Statement			XI
Concept	Jan 2014	Feb 2014	Mar 2014
Payroll deduction lending			
Interest Income- Portfolio	$172,250	$174,617	$175,630
Fee Income	$2,879	$3,453	$3,989
Comisiones DIE	$964	$1,055	$1,177
Liq anticipada	$1,914	$2,398	$2,812
Net Recoveries	$2,671	$1,816	$3,760
Net Recoveries- Institutional	$5,019	$3,666	$4,777
Net Recoveries- Expenses	($2,348)	($1,849)	($1,017)
Provision for Losses	($73,383)	($560)	($45,723)
Provision for Losses Institucional	($29,196)	$22,143	($29,350)
Provision for Losses Dependences	($44,187)	($22,703)	($16,373)
Net Financial Margin	**$81,864**	**$158,451**	**$116,608**
Origination Expenses	($17,131)	($16,659)	($8,015)
Broker commissions	($28,327)	($13,628)	($14,863)
Operating expenses	($9,158)	($11,075)	($12,266)
Operations	($925)	($970)	($1,479)
IT	($4,429)	($5,194)	($5,895)
Operating Income	**$27,267**	**$117,090**	**$81,465**
Credit cards			
Finance charge income	$1,550	$1,552	$1,400
Recoveries and CO sales	$2	$0	$0
Interest Expenses	$0	$0	$0
Provision for losses	($261)	($659)	($504)
Net Financial Margin	**$1,292**	**$893**	**$897**

- **Data association**: As discussed earlier, associating colors with metrics increases the usability of your interfaces while making the analyses easier for the users. Use this technique with caution as the overuse of color can be counterproductive.

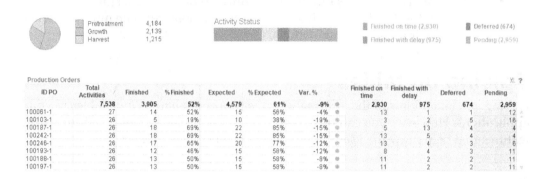

Production Orders XL ?

ID PO	Total Activities	Finished	% Finished	Expected	% Expected	Var. %		Finished on time	Finished with delay	Deferred	Pending
	7,538	3,905	52%	4,579	61%	-9%	●	2,930	975	674	2,959
100081-1	27	14	52%	15	56%	-4%	●	13	1	1	12
100103-1	26	5	19%	10	38%	-19%	●	3	2	5	18
100187-1	26	18	69%	22	85%	-15%	●	5	13	4	4
100242-1	26	18	69%	22	85%	-15%	●	13	5	4	4
100246-1	26	17	65%	20	77%	-12%	●	13	4	3	6
100193-1	26	12	46%	15	58%	-12%	●	8	4	3	11
100188-1	26	13	50%	15	58%	-8%	●	11	2	2	11
100197-1	26	13	50%	15	58%	-8%	●	11	2	2	11

- **Visual cues**: These are an old time classic in dashboard design. You can define thresholds for your KPIs and give the users a hint of how each element is doing by changing the background or font colors.

Sales Analysis - Middle Earth XL

Region	Sales 14	Sales 15	Var. %		Orders 14	Orders 15	Var. %	
	$4,846,685	**$5,154,205**	6.3%	▲	**29,914**	**32,322**	8.0%	▲
Rivendell	$371,308	$373,277	0.5%	▲	2,317	2,276	-1.8%	▼
Minas Tirith	$383,336	$363,591	-5.2%	▼	1,912	1,862	-2.6%	▼
Isengard	$334,149	$349,445	4.6%	▲	2,453	2,475	0.9%	▲
Helms Deep	$283,812	$279,880	-1.4%	▼	1,886	1,790	-5.1%	▼
Hobbiton	$244,838	$248,000	1.3%	▲	2,105	2,065	-1.9%	▼
Gondor	$266,797	$241,440	-9.5%	▼	1,687	1,475	-12.6%	▼
Gardens of Lórien	$215,291	$221,384	2.8%	▲	1,391	1,347	-3.2%	▼

Luckily, QlikView has different ways of adjusting these settings. Pick the one that best suits your business need.

The visual cues tab

The easiest way to change these formats is the **Visual Cues** tab. It lets you define the colors (**Font/Background**) and text style (**Bold/Italic/Underlined**) for each expression according to an upper and a lower limit.

Expression attributes

If you need a more complex rule to define the cell format, you can go to the **Expressions** tab and create a formula that combines multiple criteria to alter **Background Color**, **Text Color**, and **Text Format**. For example, the following calculation highlights in green all the records where the product margin is above 40 percent:

In order to define these colors, you can rely on standard functions, such as `red()` and `lightblue()`, or pick a particular RGB combination, such as `RGB(150, 30, 30)`.

Regarding **Text Format**, the options include `'<B>'` for bold, `'<I>'` for italics, and `'<U>'` for underlined. If you need combinations of these formats, use multiple tags in the same expression, as with `'<B><I>'`.

The `column()` function or the expression's **Label** are easy ways to reference a formula. This saves you the trouble of copying complex calculations repeatedly.

In the same manner, `rowno()` can help you pick particular records. It is quite useful for financial statements such as the one shown previously:

```
if(match(rowno(), 1, 3, 4, 5), RGB(255, 235, 210))
```

Custom Format Cell

Not a lot of developers take advantage of this option, but it is quite functional. If you activate Design Grid (*Ctrl + G*) and right-click on a table, you will find a **Custom Format Cell** menu. From here, you can change several parameters that will help you format your tables in an easy way.

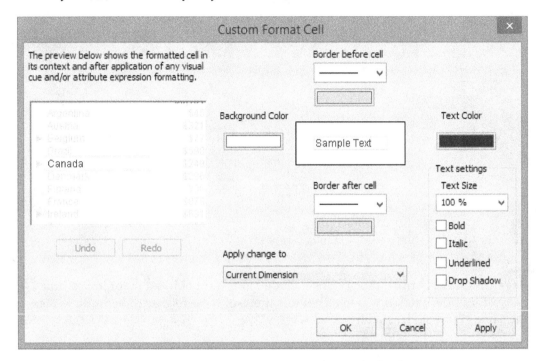

 You can make this menu accessible even when the **Design Grid** is disabled by going to **Settings | User Preferences | Design** and selecting the **Always Show Design Menu Items** box.

By using this functionality, you can create highly customized tables. For instance, you can adapt the backgrounds and borders to create a calendar-like table:

Gallons Produced: April 2015

M		T		W		T		F		S		S		T	
					1	3,424	2	2,927	3	2,856	4	2,381	5	3,028	W1	14,616
6	2,476	7	2,404	8	2,803	9	2,501	10	3,044	11	2,973	12	3,468	W2	19,669
13	2,073	14	2,130	15	2,811	16	2,476	17	3,223	18	3,050	19	3,519	W3	19,282
20	2,170	21	2,066	22	2,814	23	2,277	24	3,035	25	3,156	26	3,423	W4	18,741
27	2,138	28	2,255	29	2,845	30	3,353							W5	10,589
	8,855		8,855		14,497		13,534		12,158		11,560		13,438		82,897

Traffic lights and icons

Another trick that must be under any QlikView developer's belt is the adequate usage of icons and traffic lights. These visual cues help the users comfortably spot the most relevant elements in a table or quickly classify them depending on their performance.

Warning

The abuse of these objects can make your tables look like a Christmas tree.

Traffic light gauges

In order to transform an expression into a standard traffic light gauge, go to **Display Options | Representation** and select **Traffic Light**. It is configured just as an independent gauge chart and offers a fair variety of visual styles. Albeit that the default colors for this visualization are amazingly bright, it is advisable to neutralize them a little bit so that they are less aggressive.

Margin Analysis per Region   XL

Region	Sales	Cost	Margin	%	
	$3,562,331	**$2,988,297**	**$574,034**	16.1%	☐
Pallet Town	$1,172,383	$984,367	$188,015	16.0%	☐
Vermilion City	$329,490	$276,161	$53,329	16.2%	☐
Cinnabar Island	$319,949	$253,588	$66,361	20.7%	☐
Azalea Town	$306,240	$257,429	$48,811	15.9%	☐
Pewter City	$237,597	$190,864	$46,733	19.7%	☐
Ecruteak City	$228,332	$200,120	$28,213	12.4%	☐
Viridian City	$181,179	$156,086	$25,093	13.8%	☐
Mahogany Town	$150,677	$122,180	$28,497	18.9%	☐

Icons and images

When the situation calls for high customization, QlikView lets us display images inside a column based on a business rule. All you have to do is create an expression with a conditional statement that points to either a predefined picture (bundle) or a custom file, and navigate to **Representation | Image**:

```
if(sum(Margin) / sum(Sales) > .4, 'qmem://<bundled>/BuiltIn/led_g.
png', 'qmem://<bundled>/BuiltIn/led_r.png')
```

[Using **Relative Paths** will reduce issues when you move files around.]

Stores per Country + OMG Index   XL

Country	Stores 2014	Stores 2015	Var. %		OMG Index	
	980	1,416	100.0%		16.6%	
Germany	205	343	5.9%	↑	18.5%	●
USA	135	129	-0.7%	↓	12.7%	●
France	109	114	0.6%	↑	12.8%	●
UK	83	111	3.7%	↑	18.6%	●
Ireland	66	73	1.4%	↑	15.7%	●
Venezuela	59	64	1.1%	↑	10.1%	●
Brazil	57	122	7.8%	↑	9.9%	●
Sweden	43	41	-0.7%	↓	21.6%	●

Loading images to QlikView

When you manage your folders appropriately, there is no problem in referencing an image with its path (`'../IMG/Image.png'`). Nevertheless, sometimes you need to make your QVW files as portable as possible, so loading the images directly into QlikView can be helpful. This can be achieved by using a BUNDLE LOAD in the script:

```
Flags:
BUNDLE LOAD * INLINE [
    Flags,       Location
    Germany,     C:\Flags\Germany.gif
    Mexico,      C:\Flags\Mexico.gif
    Sweden,      C:\Flags\Sweden.gif
];
```

This is an INLINE table, but you can use any other type of data source you want (flat files, databases, Excel, etc.). After reloading, the new bundle will be available in the **Edit Expression** dialog under the **Image Folder** option.

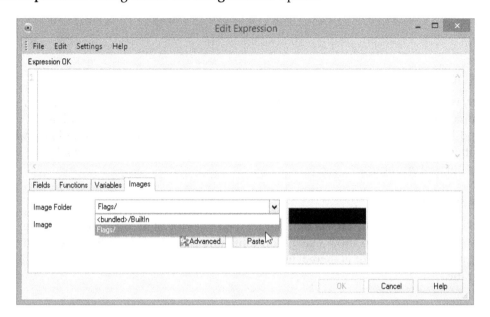

 Don't forget that loading images into QlikView will increase the size of the file.

Other visual cues

Not all visual cues have to be elaborate images or intricate gauges. Every now and then, your dashboards can benefit from putting the icons aside and resorting to old-school symbols or plain-colored cells. For instance:

```
if(column(4)>0, '▲', '▼')
```

Top Players - Mavs vs Bulls   XL

Player	Pts (G1)	Pts (G2)	Dif.		FG%	
Dirk Nowitzki	28	32	4	▲	68.1%	
Joakim Noah	12	22	10	▲	74.9%	▪
Pau Gasol	16	20	4	▲	56.5%	
Chandler Parsons	22	16	-6	▼	57.3%	
Amare Stoudemire	13	14	1	▲	85.4%	▪
Derrick Rose	12	8	-4	▼	61.8%	

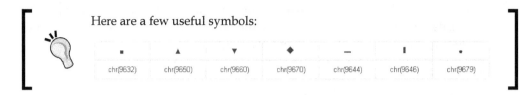

Here are a few useful symbols:

■	▲	▼	◆	—	▮	•
chr(9632)	chr(9650)	chr(9660)	chr(9670)	chr(9644)	chr(9646)	chr(9679)

Embedding charts

So far, we have talked about representing expressions as text and images. Now, it is time to bring in a new type of visualization: embedded charts. The idea behind these elements is to show a general overview of the information via trends, distributions, or the percentage of completion in order to give the users a better view of the current situation.

Sparklines

Sparklines are small line charts that depict the behavior of an element over time. Their objective is not to show exactly on which month a certain KPI peaked, but to illustrate, in general, if it is increasing or decreasing; or even if it is constant, cyclic or erratic.

Artist Performance - Last 12 months					XL
Artist	Downloads	%	Trend	Amount	PR Index
Daft Punk	60,640	57.6%		$1,783,777	16.2%
Nirvana	16,154	15.4%		$493,003	19.4%
Apocalyptica	9,624	9.1%		$306,172	16.8%
Tame Impala	8,105	7.7%		$127,357	12.8%

To create a sparkline, do the following:

1. Create a new expression with the KPI you want to display.
2. Go to the **Expressions** tab and select **Mini Chart** in the **Representation** drop-down list.

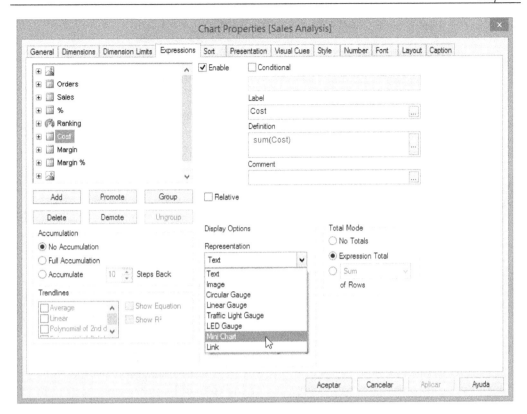

3. Click on the **Mini Chart Settings** button and select a dimension upon which to base the sparkline. Usually time dimensions such as `Month`, `MonthName`, or `Weekday` work well.

Linear gauges

Linear gauges are a great option to represent KPIs regarding completion. Whether the commercial team is pursuing a sales quota or you are monitoring a fundraising for an NPO, these visualizations let the users quickly assess how far (or close) they are from reaching the goal.

Name	Courses Completed	Courses Required	% Completed		Avg Grade
	58	70	83%		95
Sheldon Cooper	13	12	108%		100
Leonard Hofstadter	8	12	67%		95
Amy Farrah Fowler	9	10	90%		98
Raj Koothrappali	9	10	90%		95
Howard Wolowitz	6	10	60%		93
Leslie Winkle	7	8	88%		89
Bernadette Rostenkowski	6	8	75%		94

In order to create a linear gauge, perform the following steps:

1. Create a new expression with an appropriate KPI.

2. Go to the **Expressions** tab and select **Linear Gauge** in the **Representation** drop-down list.

3. Click on the **Gauge Settings** button and configure the following elements:

4. Unselect the **Autowidth Segments** box so that you can define the **Lower Bound** for each section.

5. Create two segments. The first one should start on the **Min** setting defined in step three, while the second one can start wherever you want the color to change. I will use a gray segment starting in 0 and a green one starting in 1.

6. Select **Hide Segment Boundaries** and **Hide Gauge Outlines**. This will make your visualization leaner.

Mini bar charts

This is one of the most useful mini charts due to its good readability and high visual impact. By creating a linear gauge inside a table, it is possible to simulate a horizontal bar chart so that the user can see not only the raw figures, but also a visual cue that displays the magnitudes. To illustrate it, let's work with some information regarding the top scorers in the UEFA Champions League, as shown in the following screenshot:

All-time Top Scorers - UEFA Champions League   XL

Player	Goals	/	Goals	Apps	Ratio	Clubs
Cristiano Ronaldo	77			115	0.67	Manchester United, Real Madrid
Lionel Messi	77			99	0.78	Barcelona
Raúl	71			142	0.5	Real Madrid, Schalke 04
Ruud van Nistelrooy	56			73	0.77	PSV, Manchester United, Real Madrid
Thierry Henry	50			112	0.45	Monaco, Arsenal, Barcelona
Alfredo Di Stéfano	49			58	0.84	Real Madrid
Andriy Shevchenko	48			100	0.48	Dynamo Kyiv, Milan, Chelsea

To create a mini bar chart, do the following:

1. Create a new expression with the KPI you want to display. In this case, let's use the formula sum(Goals).

2. Go to the **Expressions** tab and select **Linear Gauge** in the **Representation** drop-down list.

3. Click on the **Gauge Settings** button and configure the following elements:

4. The trick in this visualization lies in the **Max** setting. The gauge will have to span from 0 to the maximum number of goals scored by one player, so we will use the following formula:

```
max(TOTAL aggr(
    sum(Goals),      // Your KPI
    UEFA             // Your dimension
))
```

5. Select **Hide Segment Boundaries** and **Hide Gauge Outlines** to make the visualization lighter.

Tips and tricks – tables

The following section contains a series of handy tips that can help you get the most out of Straight and Pivot Tables.

Minimalistic tables

As weird as it may sound, chart junk is not an illness exclusive to charts. When some features obscure your tables instead of adding value to them, try maximizing the data-ink ratio by removing subtotals, cell borders, sort indicators, or backgrounds. Minimalistic tables can be surprisingly elegant and perfectly readable:

Performance vs Budget

▲ Baja California Sur	+ 6.4%	$2,091
▲ Baja California	+ 2.5%	$2,266
▲ Sinaloa	+ 2.1%	$1,253
▲ Durango	+ 0.8%	$318

Elements you can (but not necessarily should) remove:

Caption: Caption | Show Caption

Borders: Layout | Use Borders

Subtotals: Expressions | Total Mode | No Totals (for each expression)

Indicators: Presentation | Selection Indicators / Sort Indicator

Headers: Presentation | Suppress Header Row

Vertical borders: Style | Vertical Dimension | Expression Cell Borders

All cell borders: Style | Cell Border | Background Transparency | 100%

Backgrounds: Style | Background | Color Transparency | 100%

Spacing

Tables can benefit from increasing the cell height to two or three lines depending on the amount of data they display (**Presentation | Wrap Cell Text**). These extra pixels between records prevent your dashboard from feeling cluttered and improve readability.

> **Warning**
> Some traffic lights and embedded charts do not look so good in multiple lines.

Revenue and Expenses

Region	Revenue	Expenses	% of Sales
	$10,212,570	**$6,481,590**	**60%**
Americas	$5,602,362	$3,555,748	62%
Asia	$3,923,164	$2,489,810	58%
Europe	$668,066	$423,987	61%
Middle East	$18,978	$12,044	60%

Revenue and Expenses

Region	Revenue	Expenses	% of Sales
	$10,212,570	**$6,481,590**	**60%**
Americas	$5,602,362	$3,555,748	62%
Asia	$3,923,164	$2,489,810	58%
Europe	$668,066	$423,987	61%
Middle East	$18,978	$12,044	60%

Dimensionless tables

Creating a table without dimensions is a great way to display the most relevant KPIs at the top of a dashboard. Besides, it is much easier to maintain than dozens of text objects packed together. Just remove the subtotals and adjust the fonts and background as necessary.

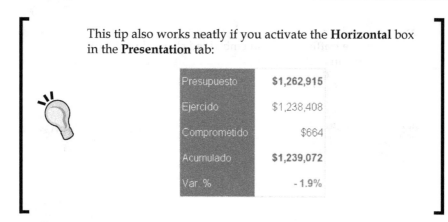

This tip also works neatly if you activate the **Horizontal** box in the **Presentation** tab:

Presupuesto	$1,262,915
Ejercido	$1,238,408
Comprometido	$664
Acumulado	$1,239,072
Var. %	-1.9%

Removing zeroes and nulls

QlikView automatically displays zeros or null values (dashes) when an expression requires it. While this behavior is desirable most of the times, you can remove these characters by replacing the **Null Symbol** with a space in the **Presentation** tab, using the **Suppress Missing** option or by changing the number format of the expression to #,##0;-#,##0; (notice that it ends with a semicolon).

Stripes

While often considered as chart junk, stripes can be of assistance when you have to deal with long tables. Even a slight contrast can help our eyes accurately read each record. Just go to the **Style** tab and add **Stripes Every 1 Row**. If you want lighter stripes (which is usually a good idea), there is a **Cell Background Color Transparency** control in the same tab.

Sales Analysis - Gotham Region   XL

Manager	Sales	%	Cost	Margin	Margin %	
Bruce Wayne	$319,949	30.7%	$253,588	$66,361	20.7%	•
Selina Kyle	$306,240	29.4%	$257,429	$48,811	15.9%	•
James Gordon	$181,179	17.4%	$156,086	$25,093	13.8%	•
Edward Nigma	$116,888	11.2%	$98,474	$18,414	15.8%	•
Oswald Cobblepot	$81,863	7.9%	$70,485	$11,378	13.9%	•
Harvey Dent	$35,597	3.4%	$29,245	$6,352	17.8%	•
Total	**$1,041,716**	**100.0%**	**$865,308**	**$176,409**	**16.9%**	

Leave the hashtags for Twitter

Though it might sound pretty obvious, it is imperative that all the columns of the table are well aligned and adequately sized. The traditional convention of text on the left and numbers on the right works well in most situations. However, some tables might benefit from centering their content; it all depends on the type of data displayed. Yet, you should always avoid overly cluttered columns. If you reduce the margins too much, you might end up with an undesirable set of pounds/hashtags that diminish the usability of the object.

Ad hoc analysis

Business users hold ad hoc tables in high esteem because they grant enough flexibility to handle unsuspected scenarios. This kind of tables allows them to create custom reports with the dimensions, expressions, and filters that they need.

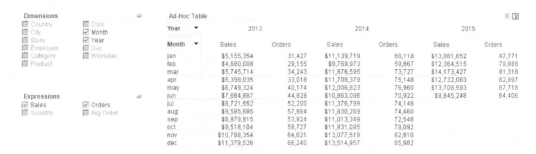

Here's how you can create an ad hoc table:

1. Create two INLINE tables in the script. They will serve as menus to select which columns to show:

```
SET HidePrefix = '_';

Dimensions:
LOAD * INLINE [
  _Dimensions
  Country
  Store
  Category
  Product
  Date
  Month
  Year
];
```

```
Expressions:
LOAD * INLINE [
  _Expressions
  Sales
  Quantity
  Orders
  Avg Order
];
```

 HidePrefix helps you hide all the selections made in fields that start with _ (or the character that you define in the variable).

2. Create a list box for each of the new fields. The **LED** or **Windows Checkbox** styles (**Presentation | Selection Style Override**) work great in this situation as the users can easily differentiate between a normal selection (the traditional green-white-gray contrast) and an ad hoc field selection.

3. Create a table that contains all the dimensions and expressions that you want to display (yes, it is a big table).

4. The magic behind the ad hoc functionality lies in the **Conditional** parameter, which will show or hide each column depending on the selections made in the menus. Let's use the `Year` field as an example. Go to the **Dimensions** tab and select the **Enable Conditional** box. Add the following formula:

```
substringcount(concat(_Dimensions, '|'), 'Year')
```

 This formula will evaluate whether `Year` is one of the available items in the `_Dimensions` field (In other words, if it is white or green).

5. Repeat step four for every dimension in the table.

6. Now is the time to perform the same procedure with the metrics. As an example, let's work with the `Sales` column. Go to the **Expressions** tab and select the **Conditional** box. The formula you have to type in is almost the same, just modify the target field:

```
substringcount(concat(_Expressions, '|'), 'Sales')
```

7. This report should only be presented when at least one dimension and one expression are selected; so, go to the **General** tab and type the following formula in the **Calculation Condition** box:

```
GetSelectedCount(_Dimensions)  > 0 AND GetSelectedCount(_
Expressions) > 0
```

If you want to customize the text that appears when there are no selections, go to **General | Error Messages | Calculation Condition Unfulfilled**.

8. To make this table even more powerful, you can add a **Fast Type Change** button (in the **General** tab) that switches between a straight and a pivot table. In this way, we can take advantage of both types of objects.

Accumulation

Even though it is not an exclusive feature, accumulation is frequently found in tables. One of its most popular usages is the **Pareto Analysis** and all of its variations, where you highlight the larger elements accumulating X percent of the total. This visualization revolves around two options contained in the **Expressions** tab – the **Relative** box to obtain the individual share and the **Full Accumulation** radio button to sum up all the previous records.

Help Desk: Tickets per Customer				XL
Customer	Tickets	Share	Cumulative Percentage	
Darth Vader	225	34%	34%	●
Jar Jar Binks	76	11%	45%	●
Luke Skywalker	57	9%	54%	○
Han Solo	45	7%	60%	○
Chewbacca	40	6%	66%	○
Obi-Wan Kenobi	35	5%	72%	○
Master Yoda	34	5%	77%	○

If the standard accumulation falls short, you can create a more robust calculation combining the `above()` and `rangesum()` functions.

Quirky tables

Have you ever faced a situation where you need to create a table but all the cells contain independent formulas? Well, here is how to do it:

Column 1	Column 2	Column 3
$13,201,445	QlikView	This is the first row
$11,057,447	16%	Hello World
$2,143,998	7.1	This is the last row

1. Create a straight table using a **Calculated Dimension**. As we want this table to have three rows (just because 3 is a good number), the formula is:

```
ValueLoop(1, 3)
```

> ValueLoop creates a synthetic dimension that goes from 1 to 3. Another alternative is to use the ValueList function, where you define the specific values for each row (as in an INLINE table):
>
> ValueList('Row 1', 'Row 2', 'Row 3')

2. The interesting part of creating these tables is defining a different expression for each row. Using a pick statement, we can list all our calculations so that they will be presented in an order:

```
pick(rowno(),
  'QlikView',
  num(sum(Margin) / sum(Sales), '#,##0%'),
  num(sqrt(50), '#,##.#')
)
```

> Combining the pick() conditional statement with rowno() allows us to create the following effect: *if you are in row 1, pick the first expression; if you are in row 2, pick the second one; and so on.*

3. Add as many expressions as you want. You can mix text with dates or other numeric formats.

4. If you need to hide the first column, go to the **Presentation** tab, select the first expression, and click on the **Hide Column** radio button.

Reducing functionality

Sometimes, it is necessary to disable certain features for the sake of usability or security. If you use column() in one of your expressions, it is advisable to go to the **Presentation** tab and unselect the **Allow Drag and Drop** box. On the other hand, if you need the data sorted in a specific fashion (for example, Pareto Analysis), you should disable the **Allow Interactive Sort** function in the **Sort** tab.

Summary

In this chapter, we discussed some of the benefits of using tables and text objects in our dashboards. Remember that these elements are vital in the pursuit of meaningful and effective applications, so don't leave them behind . In the next chapter, we will share some tips on how to enhance classic visualizations—bar, line, and pie charts.

5
Handling "The Classics"

Bar, line, and pie charts are some of the most common ways of representing data. Though originally devised by William Playfair at the end of the 18th century, these classic visualizations are as valuable today as they were decades ago. Their simplicity and high visual impact have positioned them among the most popular objects in dashboard design. Additionally, they served as inspiration to create new chart styles, such as combo, slope, and radar charts. With that in mind, in the next pages we will talk about:

- Bar, line, and pie chart usage
- Labeling and color encoding
- Best practices, tips, and tricks

About "the classics"

In previous chapters, we pointed out that bars work great for comparisons, lines are the best way to represent trends over time, and pies help us visualize parts of a whole. However, there is much more behind these classics...

Structure

The majority of objects in QlikView are capable of handling several dimensions and expressions without any trouble. Unfortunately, we cannot say the same about our brain. When dealing with numerous items cluttered in the same area, it is quite easy for us to lose focus, so try to limit the amount of data you display in a single chart.

Most of the time, keeping the number of dimensions and expressions under four will work fine (1 expression and 1 dimension, 2 dimensions and 1 expression, 1 dimensions and 2 expressions, and so on). In this regard, there are three notable exceptions. The first one refers to combo charts. Since they work with different representations at once (bar, lines, and symbols), they can handle more expressions than the average chart. In contrast, pivot tables only make sense while using multiple dimensions as each item adds a new level to the hierarchy. Finally, pie charts are only useful while working with one dimension and one expression, so they are better kept simple.

Chart orientation

Some visualizations—such as top 10 rankings—work well in either orientation. Most of the time, the decision to use a vertical or a horizontal graph has more to do with style than functionality. However, horizontal representations are often preferred because they can display long labels clearly, and you can add the values at the end of the bars without the fear of overlapping numbers.

Conversely, there are some scenarios where the orientation does affect the chart's readability. For example, when representing a trend over time, it is better to stick to the classic horizontal orientation because our brain is accustomed to reading from left to right, so it is natural for us to interpret the oldest point on the left-hand side and the newest elements on the right-hand side.

Formatting chart axes

Depending on the context of the data, it may be beneficial to remove the axes lines in order to maximize the data-ink ratio and present a leaner design to the users. For instance, the following graph already shows the values at the end of each bar, so it may be redundant to include a scale on the axis as well. In addition, the gray line between the labels and the bars doesn't add any value to the visualization, so we can delete it without remorse:

In the same manner, remember that intense colors are to be reserved for the most important elements of a chart. If you use lighter tones on axes lines, grids, and labels, your visualizations will benefit at both the aesthetic and functional ends.

Forced zero axis

It is always important to consider whether the axes will have an impact on the interpretation of a chart. If your main focus is to show a comparison of magnitudes, you should force the axis to zero (**Axes** tab). This option will display each element as big as it is and will usually make your charts look steadier. On the other hand, if you need to focus on the variances amongst the items — even if they are small in comparison to the total magnitude — it is better to let QlikView adapt the scale so that the differences are more evident.

Forcing the axis to zero in a bar or line chart is neither good nor bad; it all depends on what you want to highlight. Just watch out for charts like this one (yes, I am using a 9GAG post as an example):

Unwanted selections

Occasionally, in-chart selections are undesirable due to the nature of the expressions or the dashboard's navigation schema. If you need to disable the selections in a specific object, go to the **General** tab and activate the **Read Only** box.

Limited dimensions and scroll bars

Cluttered charts are rarely useful, so be careful when working with high cardinality dimensions (fields with many distinct values). Most of the time, it is better to limit the number of elements displayed for readability's sake. If it is enough to show only the top (or bottom) items, you can work with the **Dimension Limits** tab. On the other hand, if it is valuable for the analysis to see all the elements, it is better to add a scrollbar in the **Presentation** tab.

To stack or not to stack

Again, it all depends on your visualization's objective. Generally, grouped charts foster the comparison between individual items, while stacked representations highlight the composition of the bars. In either case, you should be careful while dealing with high cardinality dimensions as your chart might turn into an unreadable stained glass.

Changing the classic perspectives

Don't be afraid of changing old-fashioned charts with innovative alternatives that help the user better visualize the data. For example, using a bar chart with two expressions is a common way of comparing KPIs. However, if both calculations are too similar, it can be hard to see the variances over time. Take, for instance, the following graph representing the new credits positioned by a bank against its budget:

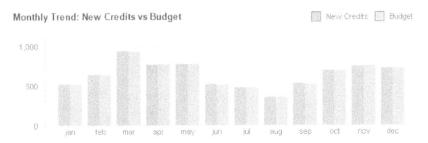

As you can see, the magnitudes are so big (and the gaps between the metrics are so small) that it is difficult to draw conclusions in this regard. If your goal is to highlight the small differences between the actual and expected figures, you can change the perspective of the visualization and plot the variances instead of the actual numbers:

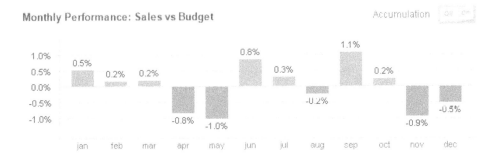

Actually, mixing both objects (maybe using a container) will give the user a better perspective of the situation. In this way, they will be able to see trends in the global magnitudes but also dive into the details and make precise comparisons.

Defending the indefensible – pie charts

If you research data visualization, you will soon realize that there are plenty of detractors of pie charts. While it is true that they have some downsides, a good designer knows how and when to use each tool, so do not throw them away just yet.

Pie charts are mainly used to represent parts of a whole, so they work best with percentages. However, as our brain is not very good at measuring areas, sometimes it is hard to distinguish which slices are bigger without the help of a legend (sorting the values can help too!). Hence, the pie chart is a bad choice for situations that require a detailed comparison.

Likewise, avoid this visualization with high cardinality dimensions. In other words, don't use it if you will end up with too many slices. If you are dealing with several small items, it is better to restrict the number of values shown by including an **Others** slice (**Dimension Limits** tab).

Number of Orders per Channel

	Online	Store
	119	252
	32.1%	67.9%

One of the hidden charms of pies is their shape. While lines usually require a horizontal, rectangular area and bar charts demand an elongated space, pie charts can adapt a little better to difficult spaces.

Top Browsers

Chrome	43%
Others	16%
Safari	14%
IE	12%
Firefox	10%
Opera	5%

Top Browsers

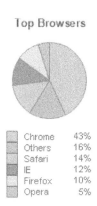

Chrome	43%
Others	16%
Safari	14%
IE	12%
Firefox	10%
Opera	5%

Albeit that it is a little difficult to master this type of chart, they are quite popular amongst business users, so it may be nearly impossible to get rid of them. Remember that there are no bad tools, only misapplications (well, maybe the radar chart IS a bad tool, but you get the point).

Special icons

Have you ever printed a QlikView object using the caption icon? Well, neither has the vast majority of users around the globe. Even though all charts include multiple icons in the caption bar by default, it is better to include only the relevant ones. By doing this, you will also reduce the chartjunk and create a leaner visualization. In this regard, don't forget that most of these functions are available through the contextual menu (that is, by right-clicking it); so, it is possible to hide most of the icons without reducing the object's functionality.

Let the color talk

When used adequately, color can greatly improve your visualization by making it easier to read or adding valuable information. There are several ways of taking advantage of colors within a chart, for instance:

- **Data association**: As we have mentioned before, using consistent colors for the dimensions and expressions across all the objects in a dashboard makes the users feel more comfortable and increases the overall usability.

> The **Persistent Colors** option is a great ally in this regard (**Colors** tab).

- **Highlight**: Just as a traffic light gauge inside a table, changing the color of a bar or slice can highlight certain elements in a chart. The Gestalt principles of consistency and similarity will immediately isolate the items in contrasting colors disregarding their size. Color functions such as RGB and ARGB are frequently used for this purpose.

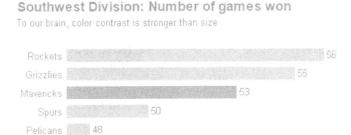

- **Using color as a metric**: Although less accurate than size or position, color can represent a KPI based on its intensity or hue. Usually, this effect is accomplished using the `ColorMix()` function.

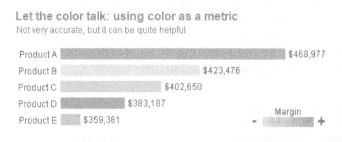

Legen... wait for it... dary

Time to talk about one of the most relevant parts of a chart: the legends. The correct usage of labels boosts the usability of any dashboard by adding context to each visualization (the type of information being displayed, units of measurement, or the base of comparison, just to name a few). There are several ways of labeling a chart, and it is your job as a QlikView designer to decide which ones to include, their position, and their format.

These are the most common ways to include labels inside a chart:

- **Window title**: It is included in the caption bar and usually contains the title of the chart. You can configure it in the **Caption** tab.

- **Title in Chart**: An alternative to displaying the chart title when you hide the caption or when a subtitle is necessary. To edit or delete it, go to **General | Show Title in Chart | Title Settings**.

- **Dimension Axis**: This represents each element of the dimension. If it is not necessary, you can hide it by disabling the **Show Legend** option in the **Dimensions** tab.

- **Expression Axis**: These are the reference numbers along the *y*-axis. You can delete them by selecting **Hide Axis** or using a transparent font in the **Axes** tab.

- **Dimension Label**: This is the name of the dimension. It is often dispensable as the dimension elements explain themselves. Change its content or completely delete it with the **Label** box in the **Dimension** tab.

- **Expression Label**: This is the name of the expression. Even though you do not see it in the chart, it is vital to include it because it will appear on the popups.

- **Values on Data Points**: These are the numbers shown at the end of the corresponding bar, line, or slice. To include them, go to **Expressions | Values on Data Points**.

- **Values on Axis**: These are the numbers shown next to each item along the axis. To include them, go to **Expressions | Text on axis**.

- **Values as Popups**: These only appear when the cursor hovers over a value. You can build new expressions to display customized messages by going to **Expressions | Text as Pop-up**.

- **Text in Chart**: Whenever you need an extra label, you can rely on the **Text in Chart** grouping inside the **Presentation** tab.

- **Reference Lines**: If you need to include a label that explains what a reference line means, check the **Show Label in Chart** box while creating it.

- **Legend**: It usually appears on the right-hand side of a chart when a color reference is needed. If you want to delete or format it, just look for the **Legend** grouping in the **Presentation** tab (it contains many appealing options).

Labeling best practices

Here are some tips that might be useful when working with chart labels:

- Add all the information required to fully understand the message behind a chart. This includes titles, axes, legends, or even explanatory text blocks for complex visualizations.

- Increase the data-ink ratio by removing redundancy. For example, if **Window Title** is enough to give context to a chart, you can omit the **Title in Chart** along with other labels.

- Avoid the vertical or diagonal axis labels when possible (their readability is much lower as compared to the horizontal ones).

- Be concise and clear. An obnoxiously long title is as bad as an oversimplified one. Avoid references like `Nt. Pr. p/Cust.`

- The titles should be located near the data, but be careful while positioning them; a selection could make your labels overlap with the chart contents.

- If possible, avoid staggering labels (**Axes | Stagger Labels**). For example, while working with dates, people can assume that the point without text between January and March is February even if it is not displayed along the axis.

Enhancing the classics: tips and tricks

In the following section, you will find a bunch of recipes that are valuable by themselves, but moreover, they contain interesting features that you can apply in many other contexts. If you want to follow the exercises (which I highly recommend), download the materials for this chapter from https://qlikfreak.wordpress.com/books/.

Twin bar chart

This graph is built with two sets of bars going in opposite directions. It can be applied in any situation where you need to compare two groups face to face. For instance, brick and mortar against online sales (*x*-axis) divided by the average ticket size (*y*-axis).

Example: Population Pyramid

Relevant features: Chart orientation, stacked bars, and cluster distance

To create this twin bar chart, perform the following steps:

1. Create a new bar chart using Age as the dimension.

2. Our first expression will represent the female population (on the right-hand side):

   ```
   sum({$<Gender={'Female'}>} Population)
   ```

3. Now, add a second expression to represent the male population. Make sure that it goes to the opposite side by forcing a negative value:

   ```
   sum({$<Gender={'Male'}>} -Population)
   ```

4. In the **Style** tab, click on the **Horizontal Orientation** icon.

5. While there, also select the **Stacked Subtype** bullet.

> The **Grouped / Stacked Subtypes** bullet can refer to either a second dimension or subsequent expressions depending on the structure of your chart.

6. Go to the **Presentation** tab and set the **Cluster Distance** to one point. This will position the bars closer to each other and give the chart a different look.

> **Bar Distance** refers to the separation between the items that belong to the same group while, **Cluster Distance** denotes the space between the different groups of bars.

7. Go to the **Colors** tab and change the first two tiles so that they become pink and blue respectively.

8. Configure the rest of the chart as you prefer.

9. Our visualization is now ready, congratulations!

Completion chart

Though it is not its main purpose, bar charts can be disguised as linear gauges. In this example, we are going to create a visualization that displays the current progress of the projects in our firm.

Example: Project Completion chart.

Relevant features: `column()`, values on data points, and plot values inside the segments

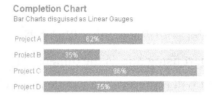

For this visualization, perform the following steps:

1. Create a new bar chart using `Project` as the dimension.

2. Add the following expression to represent the percentage of completion:

   ```
   sum(Completion)
   ```

3. Select the **Horizontal Orientation** in the **Style** tab.

4. In order to create the gray bar in the background representing 100 percent, we have to add a new expression — the remainder:

   ```
   1 - column(1)
   ```

The `column()` function lets you reference another expression in the same chart and saves you the time of retyping the whole formula time and again. In addition, it makes the charts easier to maintain as you do not have to modify two expressions if the calculation changes.

Warning: Beware of **Column Drag & Drop!**

5. Select the **Stacked Subtype** inside the **Style** tab.

6. Go to the **Presentation** tab and unselect the **Show Legend** box. This is a little side effect of using two expressions, but we have no use for these references.

7. In the **Expressions** tab, select the first formula and select the **Values on Data Points** box. This will display the figures at the end of each bar.

8. As we want these numbers to appear inside the bars, let's select **Plot Values Inside Segments** in the **Presentation** tab.

9. In this particular chart, it is not really necessary to show numbers along the axes (all our bars go from 0 to 100 percent). Therefore, go to the **Axes** tab and select **Hide Axis**.

10. In order to improve readability, still in the **Axes** tab change the font color of the labels shown inside the bars by clicking on the **Font** button at the top of the window (yes, there are two **Font** buttons).

 The top area of this tab refers to the expressions, while the bottom area refers to the dimensions. As you can see, it is possible to assign a different format (color, font, and width) to each axis.

11. Adjust the rest of the chart as you see fit and voilà! We have created a completion chart.

Dot plot

One of the most elegant charts in QlikView's arsenal — and a great alternative to bar charts — is the dot plot. It works nicely in either orientation, and you can include multiple dimensions or expressions.

Example: Gender Comparison graph.

Relevant features: Persistent colors and text in chart

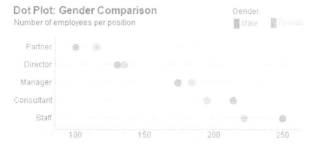

Here's how you can create this chart:

1. Create a new horizontal combo chart using both `Position` and `Gender2` as the dimensions (in that order).

2. Add an expression to represent the number of employees:

    `sum(Employees)`

3. As this will be a dot plot, go to the **Expressions** tab and change its representation to **Symbol | Dots**.

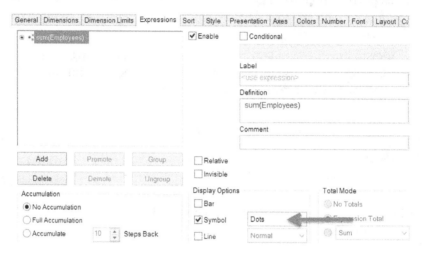

4. In order to increase the readability of this chart, go to **Presentation** and increase the **Symbol Size** to 5 or 6 points.

5. Now, go to the **Colors** tab and select the **Persistent Colors** box. While there, use blue and pink as the preferred colors in your chart.

> This option locks the color map so that every item in the corresponding dimension has a consistent color across the whole application. It is very useful for color encoding, especially while working with several objects. In this example, the 'Male' values will always be blue, while the 'Female' values will remain pink regardless of the selections.

6. In the **Axes** tab, activate the **Show Grid** option for **Dimension Axis**. This will create a light line that lets the users know exactly which dots correspond to each element.

7. Although the default legend works perfectly in this scenario, let's try another style. Go to the **Presentation** tab and unselect **Show Legend**.

8. In the **Text in Chart** grouping, click on the **Add** button and type this string:

    ▌ `Male`

9. Click on **Font** and adjust the color to blue.

10. Repeat the last two steps for the female label using pink.

11. Locate the new labels wherever you see fit by dragging each element while holding *Ctrl + Shift*.

> When you hold *Ctrl + Shift*, some red lines around the internal parts of the chart will become visible. This means that you can move and resize them.
>
> Some of these elements (particularly the legends), have a magnet function that changes their shape if you locate them near the edges. If you screw up, there is a **Reset User Sizing** and **Reset User Docking** button in the **General** tab.

12. Make any other adjustments that you see fit in order to make your visualization stunning.

13. Done! Enjoy your newly created dot plot.

Waterfall chart

If you need to visualize the impact of accumulating positive and negative movements, the waterfall chart is your best choice. It is a great way to break down total figures into their basic components and a classic chart when it comes to finances.

Example: Revenue, cost, and profit chart

Relevant features: Bar offset and color assignment

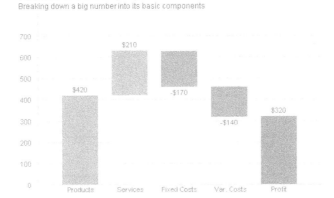

To create the preceding chart, do the following:

1. Create a new bar chart with no dimensions (yep, no dimensions at all).

2. In this example, we will create an independent calculation for each bar. Hence, we ought to create five expressions:

Label	Definition
Products	`sum({$<Concept={'Products'}>} Amount)`
Services	`sum({$<Concept={'Services'}>} Amount)`
Fixed Costs	`sum({$<Concept={'Fixed Costs'}>} Amount)`
Var. Costs	`sum({$<Concept={'Var. Costs'}>} Amount)`
Profit	`sum(Amount)`

3. The trick behind a waterfall chart lies in the **Bar Offset** parameter, which can be accessed by clicking on the **Expression Expansion** icon. This feature tells QlikView the point where each column should start.

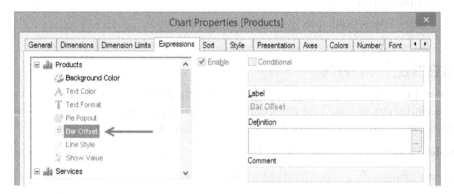

4. Add the following formulas to the **Bar Offset** parameter on each bar:

Expression	Bar Offset
Products	
Services	`column(1)`
Fixed Costs	`column(1) + column(2)`
Var. Costs	`column(1) + column(2) + column(3)`
Profit	

These formulas force each column to start exactly where the last one ended. Therefore, the first bar will start at 0, the second one will start where the first one ends (defined by the result of `column(1)`), and so on.

5. Go to the **Presentation** tab and unselect the **Show Legend** box. As we are using a dimensionless chart, the labels will appear in the *x*-axis instead of an independent legend.

6. Show the figures at the end of each column by selecting the **Values on Data Points** box on each expression.

7. In the **Colors** tab, adjust the palette so that the first two columns are painted in green, the third and fourth in red, and the fifth one in blue.

 Remember that the colors are assigned according to the order of the expression; they go from top to bottom and from left to right.

8. Make the final adjustments to improve the look and feel of the visualization. The waterfall chart has been delivered!

Waterfall chart – Vol. 2

All good stories deserve a sequel, and the waterfall chart is not an exception. Another way to create this visualization is by dynamically calculating the bar offset as the accumulation of the previous elements. Though it is not very common, it is a great way to illustrate the power of the range functions.

Example: A waterfall chart displaying the number of products in stock per week. These figures must be calculated by accumulating the items received and sold.

Relevant features: Bar offset, `RangeSum()`, interrecord functions, background color, values on data points, text on axis, and number format pattern.

To create this waterfall chart, perform the following steps:

1. Create a new bar chart using `Week` as the dimension and `sum(Quantity)` as the expression.

 This expression only portrays the weekly movements of a product (that is, the number of items that came in and went out).

2. Time for some color encoding: we will use green for when the stock goes up and red for when it goes down. Click on the **Expression Expansion** icon and type the following formula in **Background Color**:

   ```
   if(column(1)>0, RGB(172, 204, 136), RGB(255, 149, 149))
   ```

3. The next step is adding some labels. First, we will add a legend that shows the weekly movements. Select the **Text on Axis** box (**Expressions** tab). This will show the numbers right above the *x*-axis.

4. As we are displaying the products that came in or went out, it is a good idea to change the numbers' formats. Go to the **Number** tab, select **Integer** and change **Format Pattern** (the box on the right-hand side) to:

   ```
   +#,##0;- #,##0
   ```

 This string defines the formats for positive and negative values respectively.

5. The **Text on Axis** usually appears in a barely visible color, so change it by opening the **Expression Expansion** icon (in the **Expressions** tab) and modifying its **Text Color** value. In this case, a simple RGB will suffice:

   ```
   RGB(100, 100, 100)
   ```

6. Now, let's add a second label that represents the number of items available in stock. For example, in the first three weeks, we received 10, 2, and 4 items respectively. Then, in week four, we got rid of 3. Therefore, at the end of that period, we had a total of 13 items available (*10 + 2 + 4 - 3*).

7. Create a new expression using the following calculation:

   ```
   sum(Quantity)
   ```

8. In the **Expressions** tab, locate the **Accumulation** grouping and select **Full Accumulation**.

9. We don't want this new expression to be shown as another set of bars but only as a label over the existing ones. Therefore, in the **Display Options** grouping, select **Values on Data Points** and unselect the **Bar** box.

10. Remove the extra legend that appeared in the last step by disabling the **Show Legend** box in the **Presentation** tab.

11. Now, the waterfall effect. Since it is a little complex, let's clarify our objective first: we need each bar to start where the previous one ended. Thus, the total height of the bar will represent the items in stock, while the size of the bar will embody only the weekly movements.

12. Click on the first expression's **Expansion** icon and type the following calculation in the **Bar Offset** parameter:

```
RangeSum(above(sum(Quantity), 1, RowNo()))
```

 By combining `RangeSum()` with `above()`, we will simulate the **Full Accumulation** option and, therefore, define the bar offset as the total quantity accumulated until the last step.

13. Customize the axes, titles, and borders as you prefer.

14. Now we're ready to go. Cheers!

Control chart

This chart is mainly used to check how a process changes over time and to determine whether each element is under control (that is, if it's between an upper and a lower limit).

Example: Caffeine level among different product lots.

Relevant features: Reference lines, line styles, and conditional colors.

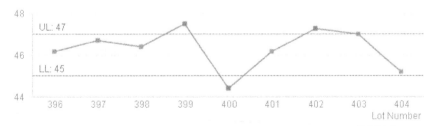

You can create this chart by doing the following:

1. Create a new line chart using `Lot` as the dimension and `avg(Caffeine_Level)` as the expression.

2. In the **Axes** tab, disable the **Forced 0** option.

 If you want a fair comparison of magnitudes, the **Forced 0** option should remain active. In this case, as we want to focus on the slight changes between the lots, it is better to disable it.

3. In order to create the control limits, go to the **Presentation** tab and add two reference lines. Even though it is possible to use variables or calculations to define them, in this example, we will just hardcode the first one at 45 and the second one at 47. Do not forget to select the **Show Label in Chart** box so that we see the labels above the lines.

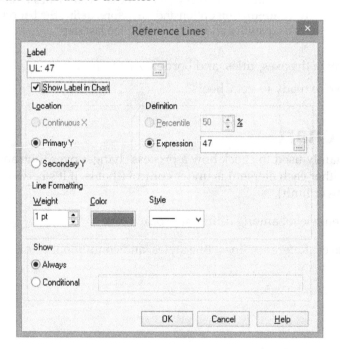

4. In order to highlight the lots located outside the control limits, let's create a new expression using the same formula. However, this time, instead of using the **Line** representation, select **Symbol | Squares Filled**.

5. Click on the **Expansion Icon** of the second expression and type the following calculation in the **Background Color** parameter:

```
if(column(2)>47 OR column(2)<45, RGB(220, 0, 0))
```

6. Even though we are highlighting all the elements out of the control area in red, the rest of the squares look odd due to their color. Let's fix this issue by going to the **Colors** tab. Copy the first color by right-clicking on its tile and selecting **Copy**. Afterwards, paste it on the second tile.

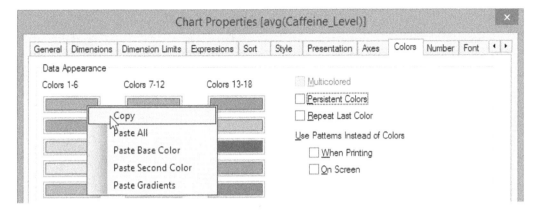

7. As usual, the default symbol size is too small, so go to the **Presentation** tab and increase it to 3 points.

8. While there, disable the **Show Legend** option. Even though we are using two expressions (one for the line and one for the squares), both calculations represent the same metric.

9. Format the rest of the chart as you prefer and presto!

Slope chart

Slope charts are a variation of the traditional line charts. However, instead of describing the ups and downs along the way, this visualization focuses on how the journey started and how it ended. It is perfect for *then and now* analyses (much like that TV show that presents celebrities and how they looked 30 years ago).

When working with these charts, our brain will easily spot patterns and recognize the distinctive slopes of certain elements (in terms of direction or magnitude). It is also an intuitive way of showing how the rankings changed from a point in time to another, as the lines will intersect each other and end up in a different order.

Example: A distribution of students and how it changed between 1990 and 2015.

Relevant features: Preloaded color formulas.

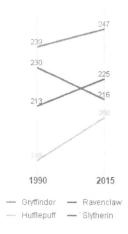

Hogwarts: Then and Now
Number of students per house

Here's how you can create such a chart:

1. Create a new line chart using two dimensions: `Year` and `House`.

2. In technical terms, the only difference between a slope and a line chart is the number of elements displayed. In this case, we only require the maximum and minimum years, so our expression would be:

   ```
   sum({$<Year={$(=max(Year)), $(=min(Year))}>} Students)
   ```

    If you need a good reference for set analysis, I strongly recommend you check out Barry Harmsen and Miguel Garcia's book, *QlikView 11 for Developers*. It is a great publication and contains an entire chapter regarding this topic.

3. In the **Expressions** tab, activate the **Values on Data Points** box.

4. As we are showing the exact values for each point, we can go to the **Axes** tab and select **Hide Axis**.

5. While you are there, disable the **Forced 0** option.

6. Finally, let's use the same color for the lines and their corresponding labels in order to improve readability (it can be a little confusing when two lines are too close). Click on the **Expression Expansion Icon** and type the following formula in both the **Background** and **Text Color** parameters:

```
House_Color
```

> Yep, there is a trick here. If you open the data model, you will see that there is a field called `House_Color` that contains a series of RGB functions. So, it is not necessary to type a complex conditional expression every time you want to assign a color.
>
> In order to create this type of field, you need to build an RGB with its three components. For example:

House	R	G	B
Gryffindor	226	82	82
Slytherin	43	132	71
Hufflepuff	230	190	0
Ravenclaw	29	111	150

→

```
House_Colors:
LOAD House,
     RGB(R, G, B) AS House_Color
FROM [..\2. Datasources\Chapter 5.xlsx]
(ooxml, embedded labels, table is Colors);
```

7. Make the final adjustments to this visualization.

8. Done. Enjoy your new slope chart!

Variance highlight

This visualization is a little twist to the Completion Chart recipe. It is also based on a gray bar that ranges from 0 to 100 percent; however, instead of focusing on the actual progress, it highlights the variance against the objective.

Example: The comparison of Sales versus Quota.

Relevant features: Conditional expressions, format pattern, and error bars.

To create this chart, perform the following steps:

1. Create a new horizontal bar chart using `Salesperson` as the dimension.

2. Add the variance against the quota as the first expression:

   ```
   sum(Sales) / sum(Quota) - 1
   ```

    This expression will not be visible by the end of the recipe. However, it will serve as a label and a reference for the next calculations.

3. On to the visible stuff. This visualization is composed of three parts: the gray baseline, the colored variance, and the error bar. The gray column is a bit tricky because it can represent either 100 percent (if the salesperson surpassed the quota) or the actual percentage of completion (if she didn't achieve the goal). Therefore, in order to create it, we ought to evaluate whether the variance (our first column) is positive or negative. Create a new expression and type the following formula:

   ```
   if(column(1)>0, 1, 1 + column(1))
   ```

4. On the other hand, the colored part may represent either the surplus (if the salesperson exceeds the quota) or the deficit (if she didn't do it). Create a third expression based on this calculation:

   ```
   if(column(1)>0, column(1), -column(1))
   ```

5. As we mentioned before, the first expression will only serve as a label, so select the **Values on Data Points** box instead of the **Bar** option in the **Display Options** grouping (**Expressions** tab).

6. Go to the **Style** tab and select **Stacked Subtype**. Also, change the chart orientation to **Horizontal** if you haven't done so.

7. In the **Presentation** tab, unselect the **Show Legend** box.

8. Now, it is time to adjust the colors. The first part of the bar will always remain the same, so you can go to the **Color** tab and change the second tile to gray (Yep, it is the second one. We do not actually see the first color because this expression is *invisible* due its representation).

9. Conversely, the second part of the chart does change according to the salesperson's performance. So, go to the **Expressions** tab, click on the third expression's **Expansion** icon and modify its **Background Color** value using this formula:

   ```
   if(column(1)>0, RGB(155, 195, 115), ARGB(0, 0, 0, 0))
   ```

We are telling QlikView to display the positive variances in green and keep the negative ones hidden using the **ARGB** function (**A** stands for alpha and 0 means totally transparent).

10. While you are there, also change the **Text Color** parameter so that the labels appear in either red or green:

    ```
    if(column(1)>0, RGB(84, 118, 50), RGB(180, 0, 0))
    ```

11. In the same manner, add the following expression to the **Text Format** parameter so that the labels are displayed in bold:

    ```
    '<B>'
    ```

12. Go to the **Numbers** tab, select all the expressions, and apply the **Fixed to 1 Decimal** format. Also, select the **Show in Percent** option.

13. Here is a little trick to enhance the labels of the first expression (the one that displays the values at the end of the bars). Let's change its **Format Pattern** to include some symbols like the ones we reviewed in *Chapter 4, It's Not Only about Charts*:

    ```
    ▲ #,##0.0%;▼ -#,##0.0%
    ```

14. Here's an interesting (and almost unknown) feature of QlikView's charts. We are going to use error bars to highlight the gap between the actual percentage and the goal for all the items that obtained less than 100 percent. Go to the **Expressions** tab, select the second calculation, and select the **Has Error Bars** option.

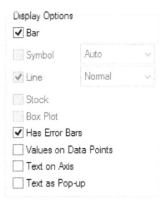

15. Click on the **Expression Expansion Icon** (still on the second expression) and add the following formula to the **Error Above** parameter:

    ```
    if(sum(Sales) / sum(Quota) - 1<0,
    -(sum(Sales) / sum(Quota) - 1))
    ```

16. Now, use this formula for **Error Below**:

```
0.0001
```

 Error Below and **Error Above** refer to the lower and upper limits of the error bars, respectively. This visual cue is based on where the main bar ends, not the axis itself.

17. The width and thickness of the error bars are modified in the **Presentation** tab. For this example, use the following parameters:

18. Now, the final touch: go to the **Presentation** tab, and add a red reference line that marks 100 percent.

19. Adjust any other visual feature you see fit, and the chart is ready to go.

Line styles

Line charts offer a wide variety of formatting options that we can use to enhance our dashboards and make friendlier visualizations.

Example: Monthly trend of operating expenses.

Relevant features: Line styles and conditional colors.

To create this chart, perform the following steps:

1. Create a new line chart using `Period` as the dimension and `sum(OPEX)` as the expression.

2. As the dimension that we are using contains a great amount of values, the labels in the *x*-axis will automatically stagger. However, we are dealing with a time field, so we can omit some of these values without much confusion on the user's side. Go to the **Axes** tab and disable the **Stagger Labels** option.

3. Create a variable that contains the current year. You can do it either in the script or directly in the **Variable Pane**.

    ```
    LET CurrentYear = year(today()); // 2015;
    ```

4. In the same manner, create three variables that contain the definitions for each year's color:

    ```
    LET MyColor1 = RGB(200, 200, 200);
    LET MyColor2 = RGB(016, 143, 205);
    LET MyColor3 = RGB(153, 216, 247);
    ```

5. Return to the chart's **Properties** window and click on the **Expression Expansion Icon** (**Expressions** tab). Type the following formula in the **Background Color** parameter:

    ```
    if(year(Period)= CurrentYear - 1, MyColor1,
    if(year(Period)= CurrentYear + 1, MyColor3,
    MyColor2
    ))
    ```

 The color usage will automatically create three line segments. Thus, we can make a visual comparison between years without losing the big picture. By the way, managing standard colors though variables is a practical option.

6. In this example, the records for 2016 are not actual figures, but budgets. In order to reinforce that idea, select the expression's **Line Style** parameter and type the following formula:

    ```
    if(year(Period) = CurrentYear + 1, '<S2><W.7>', '<W.7>')
    ```

 This parameter lets you modify the width and style of the line:
*   **Width**: Use a number between `0.5` and `8`. For example: `<W3>`
*   **Style**: 1=continuous, 2= dashed, 3=dotted, 4=combined. For example: `<S2>`

7. Let's further improve this graphic by displaying the labels that correspond to the first month of each year. In the **Expressions** tab, select the **Show Value** parameter and add this calculation:

```
month(Period) = 1
```

 The **Show Value** parameter allows you to activate the **Values on Data Points** option only when certain conditions are met.

8. Since we are only using one dimension and one expression, QlikView will not add any legends. Thus, create three labels to explain the color encoding using the **Text in Chart** grouping (in the **Presentation** tab).

9. Make some final adjustments, such as in the number format, axes, and grids. Done! We can now present a friendlier visualization thanks to **Line Styles**.

Bar heat map

The usage of color to represent a metric is not only eye-catching but also very useful to enhance classic representations. By combining position, size, shape, and color, it is easier for a designer to tell complex stories and draw a better picture of the current situation.

Example: Sales bar chart and margin heat map.

Relevant features: ColorMix wizard.

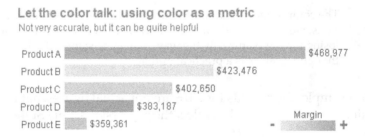

In order to create a chart such as this, do the following:

1. Create a new bar chart using `Product` as the dimension and `sum(Sales_USD)` as the expression.

2. In order to change the color of the bars depending on the product's margin, click on the **Expression Expansion Icon** and select the **Background Color** parameter.

3. Open **Expression Editor** by clicking on the **Definition** button.

4. Go to **File | Colormix Wizard**. This wizard will help you create a formula that builds a gradient based on a new expression.

5. Type sum(Margin) as the **Value Expression** and click on **Next**.

6. Select the upper and lower limits of the gradient. These tones will represent the highest and lowest values, respectively.

7. Click on **Next** and then on **Finish**. Quite simple, right? With this type of visualization, your users can better understand the product's behavior. For instance, one might realize that even though Product B is, in magnitude, considerably bigger than some others, it also suffers from a lower margin.

Summary

In this chapter, we shared a fair amount of tips and tricks that can enhance your visualizations and take your dashboards to the next level. Remember that these recipes were only an excuse to present interesting features regarding QlikView design, so now it is time to think out of the box and come up with new ideas about where and how to apply them.

Stay tuned, because in the next chapter, we will bring out the heavy guns and share some complex visualizations.

6
Creating Complex Visualizations

Most business requirements can be fulfilled with the traditional charts that we reviewed in the previous chapters. Nevertheless, certain scenarios demand more complex visualizations for a complete understanding of the story hidden behind the data. In the next pages, we will embark on a journey that will take us to a land beyond "the classics" in the pursuit of insightful and stunning dashboards by discussing:

- Histograms
- Scatter plots
- Gauges and infographics
- Geographic representations
- Overlapping objects

Histograms

One of the main disadvantages of using aggregators such as avg() is that they can hide interesting behaviors in the data. Picture the following scenario: you have access to the scores of five thousand students regarding four subjects—Science, Mathematics, English, and Literature. Each subject is graded with the help of two exams. In order to condense all these records and show only high-level figures, you decide to calculate an average. However, after analyzing the results, you start wondering: are there some extremely good students raising the global average, or are there alarmingly bad ones bringing it down? Are they all consistent? Can we separate them into groups (good, normal, or bad)? How did most of them fare?

One of the best ways to deal with this kind of questions is to create a histogram, a visualization focused on distributions instead of magnitudes. In this chart, the *x*-axis represents the exam grade, while the *y*-axis counts the number of students that scored it. As you can see, the data adopts a shape that gives us a better perspective of the situation:

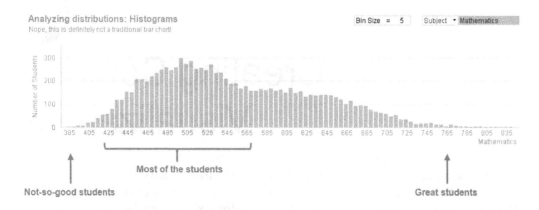

Far to the right, we can find the top students (there aren't a lot of them, but their scores are pretty high). At the other end, we find those who might need a little help (grades below 400 points), and in the middle lies the majority of pupils.

We can also appreciate that the curve is skewed to the right as most of the students have scored between 425 and 585 points. Remember, a higher bar represents more occurrences. For example, the orange bar (the highest of all the histogram) represents the 296 boys that got grades between 500 and 505 points.

Now, let's take a look at how to create this chart in QlikView:

1. Let's start by creating a histogram regarding Science. Create a new bar chart. However, this time, we don't have an existing dimension to rely on. Instead, we need to create dynamic clusters that group the students depending on their scores; so, click on the **Add Calculated Dimension...** button:

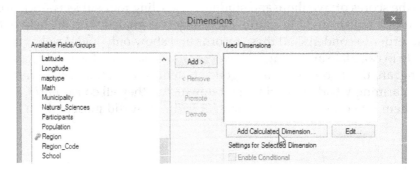

2. In the **Edit Expression** dialog, type the following calculation:

```
=class(
aggr(avg(Science), Student)
, 5)
```

> The final grade for each student is calculated by averaging the scores of two exams (midterm and final exams). Therefore, it is necessary to create a virtual table that uses `Student` as the dimension:
>
> `aggr(XXX, Student)`
>
> This also must calculate the average of both the tests:
>
> `aggr(avg(Science), Student)`
>
> Based on these scores, we must create a set of clusters in order to group the students. In this example, we used the `class()` function with a bin size of 5. Therefore, if a student scored an average of 456 points in both exams, she would be located in the $455 <= x < 460$ cluster.

3. Rename this dimension `Score`.

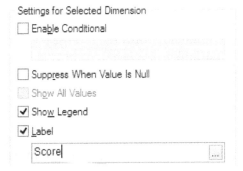

4. Now that we have created the clusters, we need to define how many students reside in each one of them. So, create an expression called `Students` based on this formula:

```
count(DISTINCT Student)
```

5. In the **Sort** tab, select **Numeric Value: Ascending** in order to arrange the clusters from the lowest to highest scores.

6. The current format of the clusters isn't exactly friendly, so let's change it for readability's sake. Instead of showing `455 <= x < 460`, we will only display the bin's lower limit— `455`. In order to do this, we need to use only the first three characters of the string. Therefore, edit the **Calculated Dimension** formula by adding a `left()` function to it:

```
=left(class(
aggr(avg(Science), Student)
, 5), 3)
```

7. Although the labels are now shorter, there are still some readability issues. Go to the **Axes** tab and disable the **Stagger Labels** option. Even though we don't show every single value, the user can accurately interpret the visualization. Besides, if a particular bar strikes her attention, the chart's popup can give her further details.

8. Albeit that our histogram is now complete, we can increase its functionality by making its parameters dynamic. Let's start by changing the hardcoded bin size (previously set to 5) to a variable that the users can edit. Create a new variable in the script called `BinSize`:

```
LET BinSize = 5;
```

9. In the **Calculated Dimension** formula, change the hardcoded parameter with our newly created variable:

```
=left(class(
aggr(avg(Science), Student)
, BinSize), 3)
```

10. We can make this variable available to the user through various methods such as a slider object or an input box. In this example, we will choose the latter, so create a new input box and add the `BinSize` variable.

11. Best practices indicate that whenever we use an input box, we should apply some constraints to ensure that the user does not get too creative with its contents. For this, go to the **Constraints** tab and edit the features as in the following image:

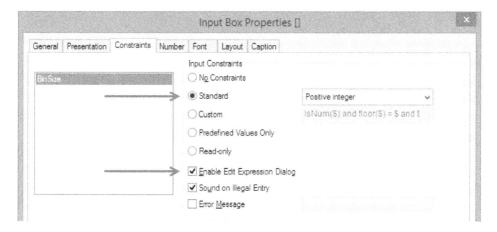

12. Change the value in the input box to see how the histogram reacts. Now, the user can change the size of the bin in order to get a broader or narrower view of the data depending on his needs.

13. Let's move on to the metric. Wouldn't it be great if we could also change the subject displayed in the histogram in a dynamic manner? Let's add a bit of spice by creating a menu of the subjects and associating it with our chart. Go to the script and add the following code:

```
LET HidePrefix = '_';

Menu:
LOAD * INLINE [
  _Menu
  Science
  Math
  English
  Literature
];
```

14. All the fields that start with the character defined in the `HidePrefix` will be treated as **System Fields**. Therefore, they will not appear in the current selections box (a desirable behavior for a navigation field like this one).

15. Create a multi box that displays the `_Menu` field.

16. Select any value (but only one item). Go to the **Presentation** tab and select the **Always One Selected Value** box.

By nature, our histogram will display any subject we want, but only one subject at a time. Therefore, it is better to ensure that this condition is always met.

17. The only thing left for us to do is to link this field to our chart; so, open the histogram's properties and modify the calculated dimension so that it references the _Menu field:

```
=left(class(
  aggr(avg($(=_Menu)), Student)
  , BinSize), 3)
```

 We added the dollar sign expansion syntax because it is necessary to evaluate the _Menu field in order to extract its contents.

18. As our dimension is now dynamic, it is a good idea to adjust its legend as well. Therefore, go to the **Dimensions** tab and substitute the **Label** text with:

    = _Menu

19. Speaking of legends, let's create a label for the *y*-axis as well. Go to the **Presentation** tab and add a new **Text in Chart** that displays **Number of Students**. Before leaving this window, adjust the **Angle** to 270 degrees so that the text appears vertically.

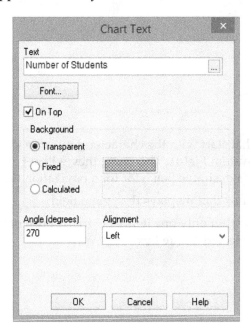

20. Position this new label along the *y*-axis by holding *Ctrl + Shift*.

21. Adjust the colors, axes, and titles to finalize this visualization.

22. Congratulations, you have created a histogram!

Scatter plots

Scatter plots are one of the strongest allies that you will find when it comes to real data discovery. These visualizations can help you find correlations, identify clusters, and spot outliers. Even though their simplest structure compares only two variables (the *x* and *y* axes), it is possible to add a third one by changing the bubble size and even a fourth one by animating the chart.

Example: **Sales vs Margin** % scatter plot divided by store format.

Relevant features: Color encoding and text as popup.

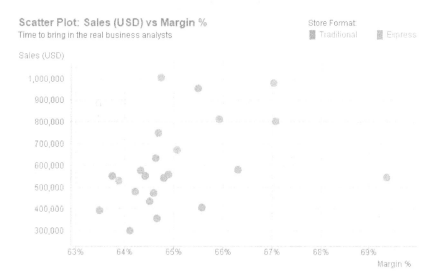

To create such a chart, perform the following steps:

1. Create a new scatter chart using Store as the dimension and click on **Next**.

2. As you can see, the **Expressions** tab looks quite different. In order to use the classic layout (and get access to a lot of useful menus), select the **Advanced Mode** box in the bottom part of the window.

3. Modify the first expression in order to represent the **Margin** % using the following code:

```
sum(Margin) / sum(Sales)
```

4. Modify the second expression in order to represent the **Sales** using this formula:

```
sum(Sales)
```

5. The resulting chart clearly has the **Forced 0** option active. In order to improve its readability, go to the **Axes** tab and disable it for both axes.

6. Go to the **Style** tab and select the sixth look:

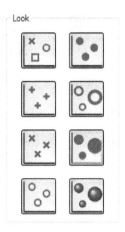

7. As the number of distinct values in the Store dimension is too big, the legend on the right side of the chart is not exactly useful. Thus, let's remove it by going to the **Presentation** tab and unselecting the **Show Legend** box.

8. Instead of this reference, we are going to create a pop-up expression with more information about each element. Still in the **Presentation** tab, unselect the **Pop-up Labels** option.

9. Create a new expression using the following formula:

```
'= = = = = = = = = = = = = = ='
& chr(10) & chr(10) & Store & chr(10)
& chr(10) & 'Location: ' & Location
& chr(10) & 'Format: ' & Format & chr(10)
& chr(10) & 'Sales: ' & money(sum(Sales))
& chr(10) & 'Margin %: ' & num(sum(Margin)/sum(Sales),
'#,##0.#%')
& chr(10) & chr(10) &
'= = = = = = = = = = = = = = ='
& chr(10)
```

 The chr(10) variable is the ASCII code for a line feed (enter).

10. Before leaving, select the **Text as Pop-up** box in the **Display Options** grouping:

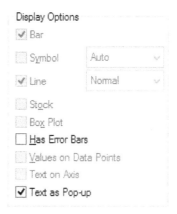

The result of this expression will be displayed whenever the user lets the cursor hover over a bubble:

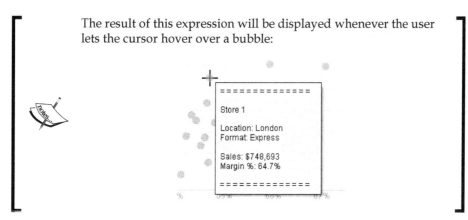

11. Depending on the size of your chart, the bubbles might be either too big or too small. If you need to adjust this feature, go to the **Presentation** tab, unselect the **Autosize Symbols** option and define the **Max Bubble Size** value that best suits your resolution:

12. As we have discussed throughout this book, you can use colors to display metrics or identify categorical values in any chart. In this example, we will plot the traditional stores in blue, and the express stores, in orange. So, go to the **Expressions** tab and click on the first expression's **Expansion** icon.

13. Locate the **Background Color** parameter and add the following calculation:

```
if(Format='Traditional', RGB(120, 198, 214),
RGB (239, 183, 88))
```

14. Adjust the axes, number formats, labels, and titles as you see fit.

15. Mission accomplished!

How to read this chart

This kind of visualization can be extremely useful to understand the business. In our example, there are a couple of interesting features to highlight:

- The higher the bubble, the greater the sales. This means that the items in the upper part of the chart are the strongest stores.

- On the other hand, the elements in the rightmost section have a greater margin percentage. In other words, these are the most intelligent stores.

- Therefore, our best players are located in the top right quadrant, meaning that they have high sales and good margins.

- In order to help the stores located in the lower-left part of the graphic, we could implement strategies to increase the sales or foster cost savings. In consequence, the bubbles would move up or right (hopefully both).

- The usage of colors often helps the user to spot patterns in the data. In this example, judging only by the position of the orange dots, we could say that the express stores are performing a little better.

- In the same manner, these representations make it easier to find outliners. Take, for instance, the rightmost bubble in our chart (Store 14: Sofia), which is clearly managing its costs more efficiently than the rest of the company as its margin is well above the average.

Color highlight

QlikView's natural behavior is to zoom in on the data once a selection is made. However, there is a great downside to doing this: you lose some context because the rest of the elements disappear. One of the most popular ways to overcome this phenomenon is to mix color functions with our good old friend—**Set Analysis**.

Example: NBA standings.

Relevant features: Set Analysis and color highlight.

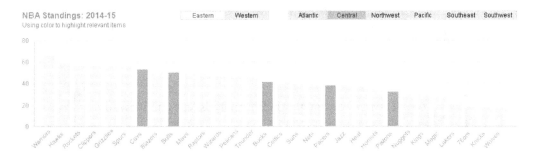

To create this visualization, you can do the following:

1. Create a classic bar chart using `Team` as the dimension and `sum(Wins)` as the expression.

2. This trick is based on two parts. First, we must work with the colors so that only the possible teams are highlighted. Then, we must ensure that even though the user selects just a couple of teams, the chart always displays all of them.

3. Let's move on to the color. Go to the **Expressions** tab and click on the **Expression Expansion** icon.

4. Locate the **Color Background** parameter and add the following formula:
   ```
   =if(match(Team, concat(DISTINCT Team, ',')),
     RGB(130, 170, 190), ARGB(45, 130, 170, 190))
   ```

This expression starts by creating a list of the possible teams (the white and green items in a list box) with a `concat()` function:

```
concat(DISTINCT Team, ',')  >  Cavs, Bulls, Bucks,
Pacers, Pistons
```

After that, there's a `match()` statement evaluating whether each team is in that list or not. If the result is positive, it assigns the bright color. Otherwise, it assigns the transparent one.

5. As you can see, whenever you make a selection, the related teams are highlighted. However, the rest of the teams disappear immediately, so our color trick will be futile unless we can force all the teams to be plotted even if they are not related. In order to do this, let's modify the chart's expression as follows:

```
sum({$<Conference=, Division=, Team=>} Wins)
```

The `Field=,` syntax in Set Analysis tells QlikView to disregard the selections made on those fields.

6. Perfect! Now, we can clearly see where the related teams stand without losing the context given by plotting the entire league.

Gauges, gauges, gauges!

We all love gauges because they are round, colorful, and mesmerizing. However, they are also the most misused object in the QlikView world. Although there is no need to demonize these visualizations, it is important to highlight when and how to use them. Here are a few features to take note of:

- These objects capture a lot of attention, so it is advisable to use them only to represent the most important figures in a dashboard.

- Gauges are not suitable for all KPIs. Before deploying these visualizations, it is better to consider whether they can adapt to the type of data that is being displayed. Really, sometimes they don't even make sense.

- Gauges are visible enough, so you can change the default colors (which are very intense) with tones that are lighter and easy on the eye.

- Their pixel-to-value ratio is very low. Gauges take a lot of space and usually convey only one or two ideas. For example, it might show 16 percent of employee turnover along with a yellow status. As a designer, you need to evaluate whether you are willing to sacrifice valuable screen space displaying a huge gauge instead of using it for a more useful object, such as a bar chart or a trend line.

- It is widely known that when a five-year-old kid learns a new word, he tries to use it anywhere and anytime until he drives everyone around him crazy. Well, this phenomenon occurs to QlikView designers as well; but instead of words, it happens with gauges. When you find a new gauge chart in a demo or a blog, there's a powerful urge to use it in all your applications. However, be careful not to force new visualizations into contexts where they don't fit. Please. Control. Yourself.

- Use a gauge style that matches your KPIs. Usually linear gauges work better for completion rates and comparisons, round gauges for ratios, and traffic light gauges to display a status.

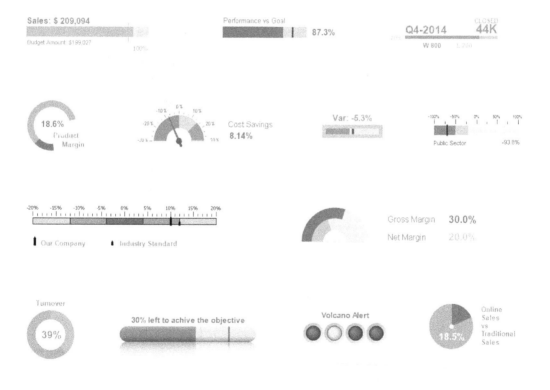

In this chapter's material, you will find several examples of gauge charts that you can copy and paste in your applications.

Geographic representations

Maps are one of the most eye-catching visualizations available in any BI tool. Unfortunately, these objects are frequently misused and end up serving only as decoration. Whether you use a specialized platform, such as GeoQlik or QlikMaps, a custom-built extension object or borrow the Google API, these recommendations might be useful while implementing geographic visualizations:

- Just as with any other chart, the inclusion of maps should be based on whether or not they add something valuable to the dashboard.

- Select the most adequate representation depending on your data. Many tools let the designer choose between choropleth, isopleth, dot, and proportional symbols maps.

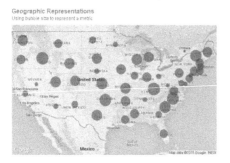
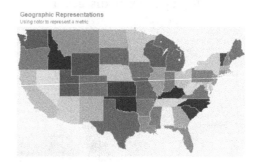

- The color palette used in these graphics should contrast with the map itself so that the metrics are clearly distinguishable from the background (no one likes to play **Where's Waldo?** in QlikView).

- Let the color talk. Even if you use a simple bubble map, you can use color encoding to represent categorical values (such as regions) or even add a metric with the `colormix()` function.

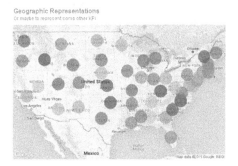

- Select an appropriate calculation. If you saw three maps representing the number of tweets, the sales amount of dairy products, and the number of car accidents, respectively, they would probably look very similar. Does that mean that most of the accidents can be attributed to irresponsible drivers that tweet on their way to the grocery store? Well, most likely not. Chances are that the most populated areas would have more occurrences of the three metrics. Therefore, these visualizations would not be as representative as you might think. Instead of using raw magnitudes, you can create composite metrics to solve this issue. For example, you could investigate the number of accidents for every 100,000 habitants.

Is that a table?

Not all tables are meant to display numbers. Actually, with a little creativity and some advanced customization, you can create amazing visualizations that will enhance your applications and give a fresh look to your dashboards.

The waffle chart

For a strange reason, it looks like most area-based graphics have something to do with food. However, this time, we are not talking about pies or doughnuts, but waffle charts. These visualizations are based on a pivot table and rely on cell customization to display a percentage.

Example: Waffle chart.

Relevant features: `ValueLoop()`, `RowNo()`, and `ColumnNo()`.

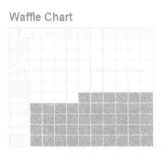

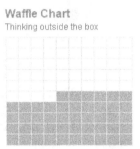

Unlike most visualizations, the construction of the waffle chart is a little unorthodox because it is based on two synthetic dimensions (that is, they don't exist in the data model) and a dummy expression. Our objective is to create a matrix with 100 cells that will be displayed in different colors depending on a metric. In order to create a waffle chart, do the following:

1. First, let's create a new pivot table using a calculated dimension:

   ```
   =ValueLoop(1,  10)
   ```

   [

   The `ValueLoop()` function returns a set of iterated values ranging from the first to the second parameters. Thus, the preceding calculation returns a list that goes from 1 to 10.
   ]

2. Create a second calculated dimension using exactly the same formula.

3. Let's move on to the expressions. Due to the nature of this chart, we will use the following calculation (yes, it's only a space):

   ```
   ' '
   ```

4. Expand the whole table by opening the contextual menu (right-clicking on the first column) and select **Expand all**.

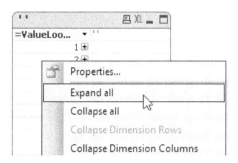

5. Drag and drop the second dimension in order to create a cross table:

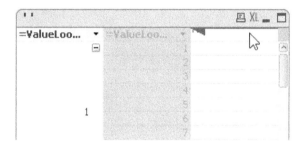

6. Now, let's color the cells based on a metric. Go to the **Expressions** tab and click on the **Expression Expansion** icon.

7. Add the following formula to the **Background Color** parameter:

```
if(((RowNo() - 1) * 10) + ColumnNo() >
(1 - avg(Waffle)) * 100      // Your KPI
, RGB(145, 180, 200))        // Color
```

The trick behind this chart is to assign a number to each cell and compare it against the desired KPI. In our case, this number is calculated by multiplying the *row number times 10 and then adding the column number*, as in the following image:

	1	2	3	4	5	6	7	8	9	10
1	1	2	3	4	5	6	7	8	9	10
2	11	12	13	14	15	16	17	18	19	20
3	21	22	23	24	25	26	27	28	29	30
4	31	32	33	34	35	36	37	38	39	40
5	41	42	43	44	45	46	47	48	49	50
6	51	52	53	54	55	56	57	58	59	60
7	61	62	63	64	65	66	67	68	69	70
8	71	72	73	74	75	76	77	78	79	80
9	81	82	83	84	85	86	87	88	89	90
10	91	92	93	94	95	96	97	98	99	100

8. Now, let's clean the chart. In order to get rid of the column headers, go to the **Dimensions** tab and type a space in the **Label** field (both dimensions).

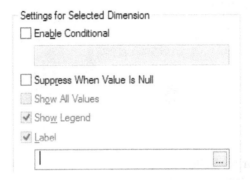

9. Go to the **Caption** tab and disable the **Show Caption** box.

10. Remember the **Custom Format Cell** menu that we discussed in the last chapter? Well, it's time to put it to use. Modify both dimensions so that **Background Color** is gray and **Text Color** is totally transparent, as in the following screenshot:

 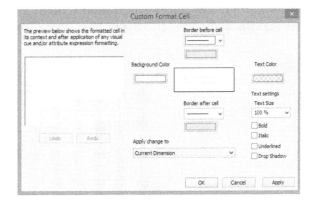

11. Adjust the columns' width as you prefer (whether you want squares or rectangles).

12. We have baked a great waffle chart. Bon appétit!

> Unfortunately, it is impossible to delete the gray cells without impacting the rest of the table. However, if you really want to remove them, you can create two white text objects to cover them.

Table infographics

Based on the same rationale as the one behind a waffle chart, it is possible to create certain types of infographics. The only difference is that instead of using color to display a metric, this graphic displays different images. Though its data-ink ratio will be shockingly low, this visualization is definitely eye-catching and might be useful for specific audiences. (If anyone asks, you didn't hear this one from me.)

Employee Turnover: 32.4%
Infographics: Every designer's guilty pleasure

Heat maps

Heat maps are one of the most interesting visualizations that can be created upon tables. They display information by coloring a matrix based on a calculation; as the color becomes darker, the magnitude behind it is greater. Though this graphic is not among the most accurate representations of data, it is still very useful to understand distributions and behaviors.

Example: A restaurant wants to spot the busiest hours of the week in order to hire more chefs and waiters so that the quality of the service remains always the same.

Relevant features: `ColorMix1()`.

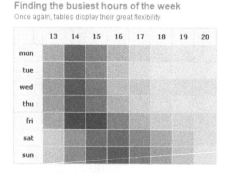

Finding the busiest hours of the week
Once again, tables display their great flexibility

In order to create such a heat map, do the following:

1. Create a new pivot table using `WeekDay` and `Hour` as the dimensions.

2. Our visualization will be based on the average number of customers per day. However, it will only be used for the background color, so let's create a dummy expression by typing `' '` (Yep, again, only a space).

3. Drag the `Hour` column to the upper border in order to create a cross table, as shown in the following image:

4. In order to give color to each cell, we will use `ColorMix1()`. This function creates a gradient between two colors based on a number that goes from zero to one, for example:

5. We know that the most intense cell should be the day/hour with the most customers in the whole week. Therefore, we can calculate the ratio we need by dividing each cell by the maximum value of the table:

```
avg(Customers) /
$(=max(aggr(avg(Customers), WeekDay, Hour)))
```

 The `aggr()` function allows us to iterate over `WeekDay` and `Hour`, so we can select their maximum value (something similar to a GROUP BY clause in the script). It is important to highlight that it is mandatory to use the dollar sign expansion here because we need this expression to be calculated at a global level and not in each cell.

6. Now, let's combine this calculation with the `ColorMix1()` function. Click on the **Expression Expansion** icon, open the **Background Color** parameter, and type the following formula:

```
ColorMix1(
avg(Customers) /
$(=max(aggr(avg(Customers), WeekDay, Hour)))
, white(), RGB(0, 70, 140))
```

7. Go to the **Presentation** tab and change the cell height by selecting both boxes in the **Multiline Settings** grouping:

8. Once again, you can hide the dimension's header by using a space as the label (**Dimensions** tab).

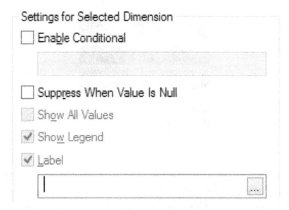

9. Adjust the column's size, alignment, and any other element that deserves your attention.

10. Done! Our heat map is now ready to go.

Overlapping objects

Most of the time, overlapped objects mean either that the designer is not done yet or that he does not hold functionality, usability, or aesthetics in high regard (and evidently did not read this book). However, there is a rarely seen third option: the charts were meticulously located one on top of the other so that together they display information in a way that cannot be achieved otherwise.

Range charts

Range charts are built with two components—a main trend displayed in the foreground and a colored area in the background that serves as the context. It is commonly used to monitor exchange rates, stock markets, and bond pricing due to the completeness of the vision that it can convey. The main benefit of this visualization is that it can show the minimum, maximum, and average values and, by comparison, the spread between its limits, all at the same time.

Example: Average temperature per hour.

Relevant features: Overlapping charts.

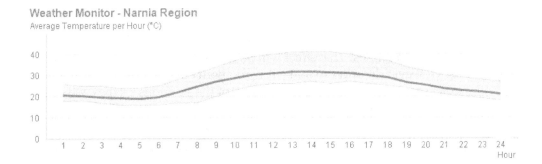

To create such a chart, perform the following steps:

1. Create a new line chart using `Hour_Range` as the dimension.

2. Add the following expressions:

Label	Definition	Line Style
Min	min(Temperature)	'<W.1>'
Avg	avg(Temperature)	
Max	max(Temperature)	'<W.1>'

3. In the **Presentation** tab, unselect the **Show Legend** box.

4. As we are only displaying one type of metric (temperatures), a monochromatic palette will work neatly. You can choose an intense color for the main expression (`Avg`) and lighten it up for the secondary ones (`Min` / `Max`). So, go to the **Colors** tab and create the chart's palette:

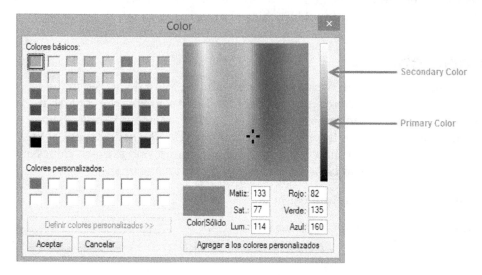

5. As you can see, by this point the only element missing is the colored area between the thin lines. This effect will be created by overlapping the two charts. However, in order to make it work, both objects must be formatted in the exact same way. Therefore, unlike any of the previous recipes, we need to do the entire tuning of the chart in the middle of the process. Take some time to adjust the titles, axes, and fonts as you prefer.

6. Copy and paste the object. From now on, we will call them the **Foreground** and **Background** charts, respectively.

7. Open the Foreground chart's properties and set the **Background Transparency** to **100%** in the **Colors** tab, as in the following image:

8. We will leave the Foreground chart aside for the moment and focus on its Background twin. Open the **Properties** window and delete the second expression (Avg).

9. In the **Style** tab, select the fourth **Look: Area Chart**.

10. As you can see, the area chart stacks all the expressions, so the top value will not represent the highest temperature, but the sum of the highest and the lowest values for that Hour. Therefore, we need to change the definition of the Max expression (which is now the second one) to:

```
max(Temperature) - min(Temperature)
```

11. Now, the two areas visually correspond to the Foreground chart. In the **Colors** tab, set the **Transparency** value of the first tile to **100%** so that the area next to the axis becomes invisible.

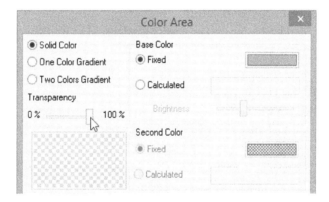

12. The second tile will look great if we use the same color applied in the Foreground chart. However, it should be even lighter so that it would not steal much of the user's attention.

 Instead of using a lighter color, you can also apply a certain level of transparency.

13. When using this kind of trick, it is vital to remember to adjust the layers so that the order of the objects does not change. Go to the **Layout** tab in the **Background** chart and set **Custom Layer** to 10.

14. In the **Foreground** chart, set **Custom Layer** to 15.

 You can use any numbers you prefer. Just remember that the higher layers cover all the lower ones. While subsequent figures work in the exact same manner, many developers prefer to use bigger steps in case they need to add an unsuspected intermediate layer later on.

15. Now, the moment of truth: overlap both objects using the alignment buttons in the design bar.

16. Now, you are the proud owner of a range chart!

Overlapping charts – other examples

Undeniably, overlapping objects is a dangerous bet. Though it can help you create visually appealing dashboards, it is rarely necessary to overload a dashboard with colors and shapes. However, sometimes the situation calls for extreme measures. These are some examples of visualizations built with overlapping objects.

Crusted line chart

This is a little twist from the last recipe. You can create a crusted line chart by overlapping an area chart and a traditional line chart with a broader width.

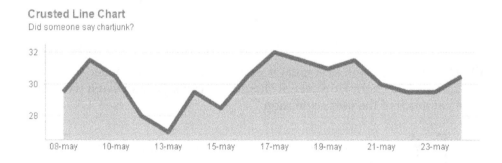

Pie gauge

Overlapping objects is not restricted to charts. You can also play with the layers of text objects and use them in multiple ways. For instance, this pie gauge is created by stacking multiple text objects, pie charts, and icons:

Area infographics

Once again, you didn't hear this one from me. If you edit an image so that its content is transparent and its background is white, you can put it on top of a bar or block chart to create an area infographic.

Extensions

When traditional charts are not enough, you can boost your dashboard's functionality by adding an extension object. These JavaScript-based plugins can create innovative and customizable visualizations that fulfill even the most detailed business requirements (and by detailed, I mean weird). Besides, the extension market will surely grow in the following months due to the introduction of Qlik Sense as a unifying platform; so, if you haven't used any of these objects yet, it's time to catch that wave.

 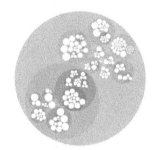 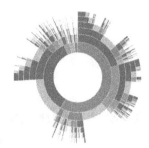

Summary

In this chapter, we reviewed some very interesting tools for data visualization. Remember to use them responsibly and always think about the information and the audience before selecting a tool. The graphics we use in QlikView must respond to the business needs, not the other way around. In the next chapter, we will talk about how to create a QlikView Resource Library in order to speed up all your developments, so stay tuned!

7
Enhance Your QlikView Experience

Even though dashboard design is not exactly a *one fits all* kind of thing, having a library of useful components to reuse in your new dashboards can save you a lot of time. After all, there's no need to reinvent the wheel every time you start a new project.

Though most developers already have some sort of base file to work with, it is a good idea to invest some time in creating a robust set of templates for your apps. This effort can be as general or specific as your context requires. If you are a member of a well-established QlikView team, it can be as simple as copying some files from a server onto your computer. In contrast, if you are a consultant or need to be prepared to face difficult situations, this toolkit will surely need to be "harder, better, faster, and stronger". The main elements to take into account in this regard are:

- The folder structure
- QVD generators and auxiliary files
- Variables
- Images and backgrounds
- Objects and expressions

This structure will help you respond to those not-so-rare situations where the business requires a prototype or a demo app in a matter of hours. Albeit that you can find some frameworks that address several of these elements, most of them are built to fit all kinds of requirements. Therefore, they include quite a few features that don't necessarily match your style or needs and add unnecessary complexity to the documents. So, don't hesitate to invest some time in creating these templates, for you will surely benefit from them afterwards.

Folder structure

Once you get used to QlikView's development style, it is easy to create new applications from the scratch disregarding its folder structure, the location of its data sources, or the overall portability of the environment. However, these elements are not to be ignored as building unstructured apps usually leads to inefficiencies and rework.

Having a robust yet simple folder structure available to start new dashboards will ensure that all your endeavors can be easily integrated with the current QlikView environment or moved around on different computers.

This structure will greatly vary from environment to environment, and it depends on the number of developers involved, the workload distribution, the complexity of the data sources, and even the personal/organizational styles. Nonetheless, it should be able to handle several applications (not only different modules, but also different versions of each one of them), a layered QVD structure (files and generators), general files (xls, txt, html, csv), images (backgrounds, cover pages, icons, visual cues), and documentation in the simplest manner possible.

> The **QlikView Deployment Framework** (available on Qlik Community) is a great reference in this regard.

Opening and closing scripts

Chances are that most of your dashboards share some features such as variables, colors, and even some visual cues. To ensure that all the apps in the QlikView environment are consistent, and to save some valuable time, you can create standard text files to use them as opening and closing scripts. These files can collect shared functionality, such as:

- Environmental and format variables
- Connection strings
- Frequently used variables such as vToday or vCurrentYear
- Standard color variables (RGB codes)
- Subroutines
- Section access
- Commonly used statements such as HidePrefix or NullAsValue

You can easily import these files in all your apps by going to **Insert |
Include Statement**.

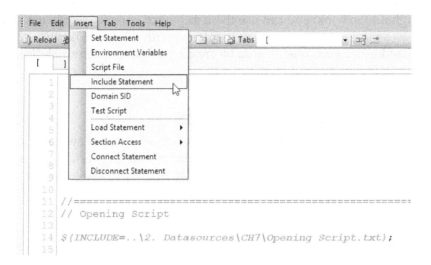

Subroutines

Subroutines are small chunks of code that you can easily include in your apps
to automate common actions. As they are built using QlikView script, they can
perform a wide variety of actions, and their ability to receive parameters makes
them very flexible.

In this chapter's material, you can find an example that includes three bonus
subroutines:

- **StoreQVD**: This subroutine stores a table in QVD. Afterwards, it drops the
  table and keeps some useful metadata, such as the number of records and the
  time spent loading each element.

- **ImageBundleLoad**: Instead of creating an inline table with all the images
  you need in your dashboard, arrange them in a single folder (it can contain
  several subfolders), and load them automagically with this subroutine (no,
  that's not a typo).

- **LoadVariables**: Using the **Variable Overview** window to create all the
  variables in the document can be troublesome and sometimes give you nasty
  surprises (if you are a seasoned QlikView developer, you have surely erased
  your variables by accident at least once). This subroutine lets you load all the
  variables defined in an Excel file so that you have a better control over them.

Variables – making your life easier

Variables are one of the most flexible elements in the QlikView realm. As we have seen throughout the book, you can use them as part of your script, the navigation schema or as a mechanism for the user to interact with the app. Likewise, they can help you standardize your dashboards by creating consistent color palettes or speed up your development by making it easier to create new calculations.

Formulas and Set Analysis

Stunning dashboards are not only functional, user friendly, and eye catching, but also robust and easy to maintain. One of the benefits of using variables in a QlikView app is that you can encapsulate common calculations. For example, imagine that you are dealing with an expression such as this one:

```
=sum({$<Category={'A', 'B', 'C'}, Cancelled={0}>} Sales)
```

Instead of copying and pasting it onto several charts time and again, you can create a variable called vSales to store it. Now, whenever you need to use it, you just have to type the variable name:

```
=money(vSales)
```

In the same manner, those terrifying 30-line expressions can be greatly simplified by using multiple variables:

```
=money(vSales -vCOGS - vOtherIncome)
```

Besides the obvious advantage of using a single variable instead of a long and complex formula, whenever the business rule changes, you only need to modify the variable definition once instead of changing dozens of objects, thus reducing the maintenance time and avoiding mistakes.

Another way of using variables to make your expressions simpler is to store bits and pieces to mix them up later on. For instance, the following variable contains the part of a Set Analysis expression that ignores all the selections made in the Calendar fields.

```
LET Ignore_Calendar =
'Year=, Month=, Day=, MonthName=, Date=, Date_ID=';
```

You can combine it with other common variables to display the YTD sales:

YTD Sales (16-aug-15)   XL

Employee	YTD Sales
	$2,046,448
Natasha Romanoff	$513,740
Tony Stark	$449,730
Steve Rogers	$447,349
Clint Barton	$333,027
Peter Parker	$302,603

Original Formula:
sum({$<$(Ignore_Calendar),
Year={$(vCurrentYear)}, Date_ID={"<=$(vToday)"}>} Sales)

When QlikView evaluates it:
sum({$<Year=, Month=, Day=, MonthName=, Date=, Date_ID=,
Year={2015}, Date_ID={"<=42267"}>} Sales)

Alternatively, you can create a custom report using slider/calendar objects linked to other variables:

Sales (16-jul-15 to 16-aug-15)   XL

Employee	Ad-Hoc Sales
	$391,525
Steve Rogers	$73,443
Peter Parker	$70,921
Clint Barton	$63,362
Matt Murdock	$50,419
Bruce Banner	$41,935
Tony Stark	$35,145
Natasha Romanoff	$23,147

From: 16/07/2015   To: 16/08/2015

Original Formula:
sum({$<$(Ignore_Calendar),
Date_ID={">=$(From_Date)<=$(To_Date)"}>} Sales)

When QlikView evaluates it:
sum({$<Year=, Month=, Day=, MonthName=, Date=, Date_ID=,
Date_ID={">=42235<=42266"}>} Sales)

> The easiest way to debug this kind of formulas is to create a nameless expression in a straight table and let the cursor hover over the column's header:
>
> YTD Sales (16-aug-15)   XL
>
> | Employee | sum({$<Year=, Month=, Day=, MonthName=, Date=, Date_ID=, Year={2015}, Date_ID={"<=42232"}>} Sales) |
> | --- | --- |
> | Natasha Romanoff | $513,740 |
> | Tony Stark | $449,730 |
> | Steve Rogers | $447,349 |
> | Clint Barton | $333,027 |
> | Peter Parker | $302,603 |

Handling colors with variables

Managing colors can be really annoying if your palette grows beyond five elements or if you need to keep consistency across multiple documents. Remembering all the codes, using Sticky Notes, or opening old files to copy the color tiles can be removed from your task list if you store them directly in variables:

```
LET Green_Background = RGB(225, 250, 225);
LET Red_Background   = RGB(255, 240, 230);
```

Then, you need to call them in the object's properties:

```
if([Margin %]>.21, $(Green_Background), $(Red_Background))
```

Besides defining a variable for the color as a whole, you can also create an Excel file that contains their R, G, and B components to assemble them later. This allows you to adjust the transparency (the **Alpha** parameter of the **ARGB** function) depending on where you plan to use them:

Backgrounds

Using an adequate background can improve the aesthetics, quadrature, and style of a dashboard. In this regard, having some designs ready beforehand can save you valuable development time.

Building a background doesn't necessarily require spending hours on specialized tools such as Illustrator, Photoshop, or InDesign. You can start your background collection by borrowing some of the images used in Qlik's demos and making small adjustments.

Start by downloading a demo from `http://us-b.demo.qlik.com/`, remove all the objects, and print the screen in order to create a base image:

After this, you can modify bits and pieces, such as the headers, panels, or shadows. For instance, you could Google *deep blue wallpaper* to get a good-looking texture, crop a rectangle, and paste it over the color stripe of the base image in order to change its look and feel to match your organization's corporate colors (Pablo Picasso and Frida Kahlo would be jealous of such talent for the visual arts!)

Also, you can isolate the raw materials of the background and save them as separate files to create a library of components that you can mix and match later on. For example, here's a collection of side images that I use for my applications:

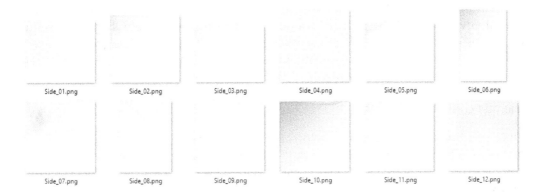

As time goes by, you will find yourself expanding your library from design websites, referring to more demos, or even creating your own components when inspiration strikes.

Icons, symbols, and buttons

Once again, the **QlikView Developer Toolkit** (available on Qlik Community) can be a good starting point to assemble an image collection for your dashboards. However, chances are that after a few weeks you will need more specific icons, symbols, and buttons to enhance your applications. If that is the case, there are several websites such as http://dryicons.com/ and https://www.iconfinder.com/ where you can download amazing packs with a freeware license.

Color palettes

For those who come from a graphic design background, mixing and matching colors is a straightforward activity. However, if you are more familiarized with programming or databases, creating a simple palette can be a titanic task. However, even if you have an awful sense of fashion, you can still be a great QlikView designer by relying on the experts. As we discussed in *Chapter 2, All about Dashboard Design Best Practices*, there are many amazing websites that can help you create an adequate color palette, so don't hesitate to visit them! From specialized graphic design websites to fashion or interior design resources, there is no excuse for not having a friendly color scheme.

Once you find the perfect mix of colors, be sure to add it to your library. You can use text objects to easily copy and paste the RGB formula or simple charts to move the palette as a whole with the **Format Painter** tool. In the end, these resources not only give consistency to your apps, but also endow them with your own style.

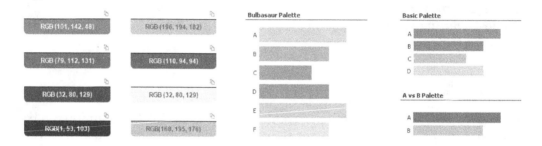

 These colors can also be stored in an Excel file using the RGB codes in order to build color schemes that can be easily imported to a new QlikView document via variables.

The object repository

Having a single QlikView file that contains several commonly used visualizations can also save you a great amount of time while building new apps. Even though you can copy and paste objects from multiple documents, compiling them in just one place (an application that will surely deserve a place in your **Favorites** side bar) is better than opening and closing dozens of applications to find that awesome gauge you created months ago.

This repository can contain specific tabs for each chart type, common buttons, maps color palettes, or even small chunks of code that might come in handy afterwards (for... each statements, set analysis, ad hoc conditions, calendars, and so on.)

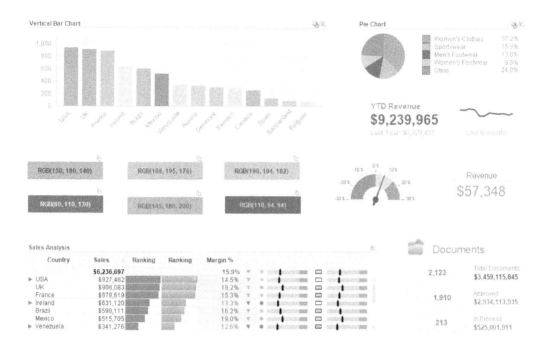

Keeping in shape

A great designer must always be at the top of his game, and one of the best ways to achieve this is to stay in touch with the global community of QlikView enthusiasts. In this regard, I recommend you to frequently refer to these resources:

- **Qlik Community**: Qlik's official portal offers a wide variety of options to stay updated, such as forums, tutorials, blogs, and demos. This website is definitely a bookmark you should have in your web browser.

- **Independent blogs**: There's a lot going on in the QlikView world outside of Qlik Community. Scattered around the globe, there are several renowned experts sharing their knowledge about scripting, design, and best practices in their personal blogs.

> Visit Steve Dark's website, `http://www.askqv.com/`, to find the cream of the crop of QlikView blogs.

- **Other Resources**: You can also benefit from joining the discussions regarding QlikView on LinkedIn, following some Qlik-personalities in Twitter or attending to specialized events such as the Masters Summit for QlikView.

- **Other platforms**: There's no harm in checking what other companies are doing every now and them. Websites and demos from other platforms such as Tableau, Spotfire, and Birst can help you get some inspiration to create new visualizations in QlikView.

Summary

In this chapter, we reviewed the main components of a QlikView library, a comprehensive repository that can standardize and speed up all your QlikView developments. In the next and final chapter, we will discuss some recommendations you might take into account before deploying an application in order to ensure that it gets the best results possible.

8

Before You Go

In the previous chapters, we discussed how to build a dashboard that is not only engaging, but also functional, maintainable, and easy to use so as to promote insights that derive in tangible value for the business. Now, it is time to talk about the activities that should be undertaken before the official release of the app in order to ensure that everything is okay. Throughout this final chapter, we will discuss:

- Activities before the rollout
- The 10 commandments of QlikView design
- After the *go-live*

Before the rollout

You have built an amazing dashboard in QlikView, and you are ready to publish it. However, before your masterpiece sees the light, some deeds must be done, and these are explained in the following sections.

Locking objects

Before finishing an application, it might be a good idea to lock the objects in order to prevent the users from moving or resizing them. You can accomplish this chart by chart by going to the **Layout** tab and unselecting the **Allow Move / Size** box:

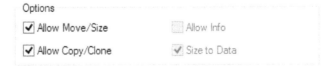

If you want to lock all the objects inside a sheet, it is easier to open the **Sheet Properties** window and go to the **Security** tab. Here, you can restrict not only the **Move/Size** privilege, but also some others such as **Remove Sheet** or **Remove Sheet Objects**:

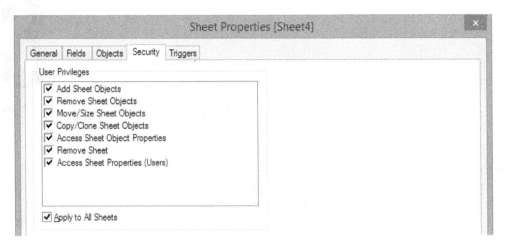

 If you need to replicate this security schema in all the sheets in the document, just select the **Apply to All Sheets** box before clicking on **Apply**.

Though locking all the objects at once is clearly more comfortable for the designer, leaving this feature active in certain charts can be beneficial for the users. Take for instance the following dashboard:

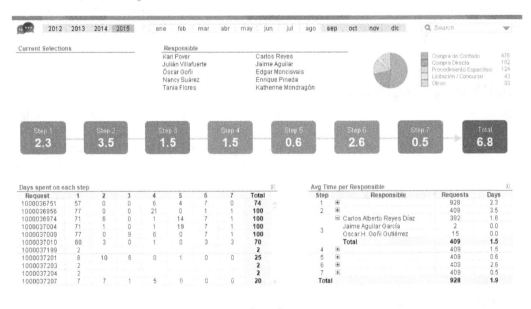

Locking the objects in the upper part of the dashboard ensures that the filters and the process chain built with text objects always remain the same. However, if the user is working on a bigger screen, he might benefit from resizing the two tables at the bottom in order to see more elements, so it is better to leave these objects unrestricted.

The application datasheet

While wrapping up a QlikView dashboard, don't forget to create an application datasheet with useful information about the data sources such as the reload frequency, common abbreviations, business rules, or KPI calculation criteria. This sheet can help the users better understand the dashboard and make the most out of their QlikView experience:

Intro	Dashboard	Diagnosis	Comparative Analysis	About

About this application and data

Data	Data Source	The data is from http://www.cms.gov and for 2011. CMS Medicare Provider Analysis and Review (MEDPAR) inpatient data which contains discharge information for 100% of Medicare fee-for-service beneficiaries using hospital inpatient services
	Spending Measures	This application presents the provider's average total covered charges and average total payments within DRG. Total payments consist of Medicare payments, beneficiary cost-share payments, and coordination of benefit payments.
	Study Population	Medicare Inpatient Prospective Payment System (IPPS) providers within the 50 United States and District of Columbia with a known Hospital Referral Region (HRR) who are billing Medicare fee-for-service beneficiaries for the top 100 DRGs. The top 100 DRGs are determined by the number of discharges.
Definition	Average Covered Charges	The provider's average charge for services covered by Medicare for all discharges in the DRG. These will vary from hospital to hospital because of differences in hospital charge structures.
	Average Total Payments	The average of Medicare payments to the provider for the DRG including the DRG amount, teaching, disproportionate share, capital, and outlier payments for all cases. Also included in Total Payments are co-payment and deductible amounts that the patient is responsible for and payments by third parties for coordination of benefits
	Total Discharges	The number of discharges billed by the provider for inpatient hospital services
	DRG	Code and description identifying the DRG. DRGs are a classification system that groups similar clinical conditions (diagnoses) and the procedures furnished by the hospital during the stay
Application	Provider	This application was provided by Infozone, QlikView Partner. If you have any questions, please contact them directly at infozoneus.com

infozone

QlikView

In-chart help

Speaking of enhancing the user's experience, it is also advisable to include help texts wherever they are necessary. This feature allows the designer to add notes about the calculations or other business rules in any chart:

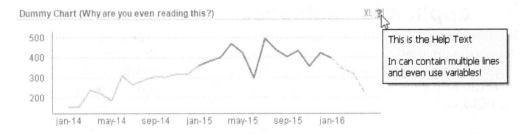

In order to add this icon to an object, just go to the **Caption** tab and type out your comments in the **Help Text** field:

The dashboard cover

You cannot judge a book by its cover, but have your ever heard anyone complain about having a nice coating? Before releasing a QlikView document, take a minute to create an image so that, instead of having barely visible snapshots of the first sheet as the thumbnail, you have representative icons that help the users easily spot the dashboard they are looking for in the **AccessPoint**:

When you need to define the document thumbnail, navigate to **Settings** | **Document Properties** | **Opening** and select **Image**, as shown in the following screenshot:

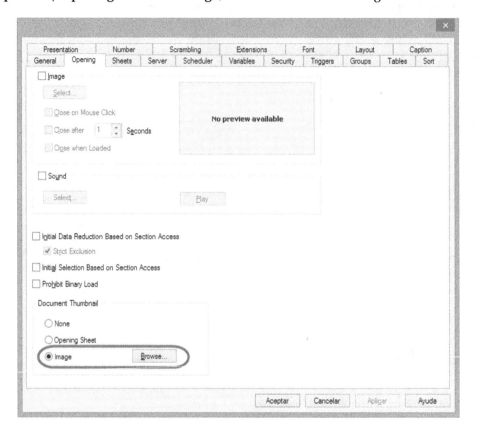

Dashboard testing

There are quite a lot of recommended tests to be performed before deploying an application. However, when it comes to QlikView Dashboard Design, these cannot be forgotten:

- **App performance**: The goal of this test is to assess how your new dashboard behaves in the **Access Point**. Several times, the performance varies between the development and production environments, so it is better to ensure that all the objects are displayed within a reasonable amount of time (no one likes to wait several minutes for a pivot table to load). In addition, if you use the AJAX client—which is advisable due to some awesome features such as session collaboration and extension objects—ensure that you double-check whether all the objects are working properly. On occasions, certain elements don't work or look exactly the same in QlikView or the IE plugin and AJAX, so some minor tweaks might be necessary to tune up your design or regain full functionality.

IE Plugin			AJAX		

Start Date: End Date:
20/11/2014   ▾ 🗓   20/11/2014   ▾ 🗓

Start Date: End Date:
20/11/2014   ▾ 🗓   20/11/2014   ▾ 🗓

Select a KPI:
☐ Sales   ☐ Margin   ☐ Cust. Retention
☐ Cost   ☐ Turnover   ☐ ROI

Select a KPI:
☐ Sales   ☐ Turnover
☐ Cost   ☐ Cust. Retention
☐ Margin   ☐ ROI

- **Usability tests**: These evaluations go further than just gathering some opinions about a dashboard and can be real eye-openers for designers. In order to create a truly stunning dashboard, you must realize how the users understand and interact with it so that you can make all the necessary adjustments to improve its navigation, data distribution, and ease of use. It is advisable to undertake multiple tests throughout the development so that you can identify the problems early and reduce the chances of rework.

  While conducting these evaluations, pay special attention to how the user approaches the dashboard and interacts with each object (what he expects, what he gets, and what he does afterwards). It is also important to take note of the most (and least) used filters and charts in order to maximize the screen usage. In the end, take some time to ask the user about the story that the dashboard told her or the conclusions that could be drawn out of it. Thus, you can ensure that the information is clear and that there aren't any misleading visualizations.

- **Number validation**: This might not be directly related to the dashboard's design, but it certainly has a great impact on the user's acceptance level. While in the early stages of the development you can work with dummy or not-so-accurate data, before the application is released, every single figure must be validated. The dashboard's structure, navigation schema, filters, and well-applied visualizations will be completely futile if the information displayed is wrong. Additionally, once an app is released and the users realize that the data isn't accurate, the road to regain their trust will be long and thorny; so, it is better to take one or two extra days before the rollout to ensure the quality of the data.

 Checking the **Subset Ratio** and **Information Density** values in **Table Viewer** is also a good way to ensure that an application is ready to go.

Documentation and backups

They are not exactly the most fun activities that a QlikView expert could undertake, but they are indisputably relevant to maintaining a robust environment. Every time a dashboard is on the verge of being released, ensure that you back up the previous versions and write the corresponding documentation.

The 10 commandments of QlikView design

Before releasing an app, double-check that you've followed the 10 commandments of QlikView design (they don't start with *thou shalt*, but they are important nonetheless):

1. Your audience and their needs are always the primary focus.
2. Let the data displayed in your dashboard tell a story.
3. Use the right visualizations to display the right KPIs.
4. Always give context to the data to improve the decision-making process.
5. Dashboard design is about enhancing the user experience and fostering discoveries, not only about aesthetics.
6. If you don't really need it, don't use it. Be simple, clear, and precise.
7. Maximize the data-ink ratio; avoid chartjunk.
8. Do not overload the dashboard; use the white space wisely.
9. Strive for simple and elegant interfaces. Never forget balance, consistency, and alignment.
10. Put the utmost care into even the tiniest details.

After the rollout

Now, let's break on through to the other side and discuss some recommended activities after the application's rollout.

Sell it!

Unlike other platforms such as ERP or CRM systems, the adoption of dashboards is — to a certain point — optional as the users may not rely on QlikView to make decisions or analyze data. Therefore, one of your top priorities after the rollout is to promote your new application among the stakeholders and highlight the benefits of using it.

Most of the time, this is an easy task because by the end of development, it is likely that you already have one or two people waiting eagerly to use the dashboard they saw in a review meeting or a usability test. So, identify your champions and work with them to position the new dashboard as one of the most valuable platforms in the company.

Dashboard navigation course

The impact of a new application will always be greater if the users know how it works from the very beginning. Despite being well designed, dashboards usually require a small navigation course where you describe the data sources, the KPIs, and its main features so that the users become familiar with it. If you use well-known structures (classic charts) it might be unnecessary to give detailed explanations. However, if you have introduced a new or complex visualization, it is advisable to take a minute to explain how to interpret it.

In addition, this might be the first approach to QlikView for some of them. If this is the case, it is important to introduce the platform, the associative model, and some general notions, such as how to make or clear selections, export objects, or create bookmarks.

This kind of sessions often increases user acceptance and fosters the dashboard's usage, making it a valuable asset in the IT portfolio.

Maintenance

QlikView applications are never truly finished; they are entities that tend to grow and evolve as the business demands it. Hence, the *go live and go home* approach is rarely applicable to this kind of endeavors.

In order to create a healthy QlikView environment in your company, it is important to take some time out to undertake continuous reviews to ensure that the information displayed in the dashboards is valid and responds to the current business needs.

Summary

In this chapter, we reviewed some tips that will help you during the dashboard's rollout. Even though these activities go beyond the traditional scope of a project, they usually improve user acceptance and contribute to the growth of the overall QlikView environment in the long run.

Throughout this book, we demonstrated that creating a dashboard is much more than just packing a couple of charts together. Instead, it is a process that requires a deep understanding of the business and its information needs in order to create insightful and engaging visualizations that foster discoveries. May you find these tips useful and apply them in your own applications. Thanks for taking the time to read this book. I sincerely hope that you enjoyed this journey as much as I did. Good luck!

Index

E

expression attributes, tables
  about 61
  Custom Format Cell 62
extensions 134

F

Favorites bar 37
filter panes 39
filter presentation
  about 40-42
  list box 40
  multi box 40
  search object 40
folder structure 136
fonts, dashboard style 32
frames 49

G

gauges 118-120
general navigation
  about 46
  logos 48
  objects, displaying 47
  objects, hiding 47
  tab row 47
geographic representations 120, 121
Gestalt principles
  about 14
  closure 14
  connection 14
  continuity 14
  enclosure 14
  proximity 14
  similarity 14
Google Search bar 37

H

handcrafted dashboards 58
heat map 126-128
hidden filter pane 42-45
hierarchies
  creating 52
histograms 107-113

I

iconfinder
  URL 141
icons 49, 141
images
  about 49
  loading, to QlikView 64, 65
independent blogs 143

K

Key Performance Indicator (KPI)
  about 5
  displaying 50, 51
  metrics, selecting 6
  selecting 5
KPI display
  about 49
  creating 56

L

layout 37-39
linear gauges
  about 67
  creating 68
line charts
  about 23, 102
  advantages 23
  creating 103, 104
  styles 102
list box 40
logos 48

M

mini bar chart
  about 68
  creating 69
minimalistic tables 70
multi box 40

N

Non-Data-Ink 16

Thank you for buying

Creating Stunning Dashboards with QlikView

About Packt Publishing

Packt, pronounced 'packed', published its first book, *Mastering phpMyAdmin for Effective MySQL Management*, in April 2004, and subsequently continued to specialize in publishing highly focused books on specific technologies and solutions.

Our books and publications share the experiences of your fellow IT professionals in adapting and customizing today's systems, applications, and frameworks. Our solution-based books give you the knowledge and power to customize the software and technologies you're using to get the job done. Packt books are more specific and less general than the IT books you have seen in the past. Our unique business model allows us to bring you more focused information, giving you more of what you need to know, and less of what you don't.

Packt is a modern yet unique publishing company that focuses on producing quality, cutting-edge books for communities of developers, administrators, and newbies alike. For more information, please visit our website at www.packtpub.com.

About Packt Enterprise

In 2010, Packt launched two new brands, Packt Enterprise and Packt Open Source, in order to continue its focus on specialization. This book is part of the Packt Enterprise brand, home to books published on enterprise software – software created by major vendors, including (but not limited to) IBM, Microsoft, and Oracle, often for use in other corporations. Its titles will offer information relevant to a range of users of this software, including administrators, developers, architects, and end users.

Writing for Packt

We welcome all inquiries from people who are interested in authoring. Book proposals should be sent to author@packtpub.com. If your book idea is still at an early stage and you would like to discuss it first before writing a formal book proposal, then please contact us; one of our commissioning editors will get in touch with you.

We're not just looking for published authors; if you have strong technical skills but no writing experience, our experienced editors can help you develop a writing career, or simply get some additional reward for your expertise.

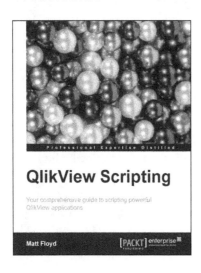

QlikView 11 for Developers

ISBN: 978-1-84968-606-8   Paperback: 534 pages

Develop Business Intelligence applications with QlikView 11

1. Learn to build applications for Business Intelligence while following a practical case -- HighCloud Airlines. Each chapter develops parts of the application and it evolves throughout the book along with your own QlikView skills.

2. The code bundle for each chapter can be accessed on your local machine without having to purchase a QlikView license.

3. The hands-on approach allows you to build a QlikView application that integrates real data from several different sources and presents it in dashboards, analyses and reports.

Mastering QlikView

ISBN: 978-1-78217-329-8   Paperback: 422 pages

Unleash the power of QlikView and Qlik Sense to make optimum use of data for Business Intelligence

1. Let QlikView help you use Business Intelligence and data more effectively.

2. Learn how to use this leading BI solution to visualize, share and communicate insights.

3. Discover advanced expressions and scripting techniques that will help you get more from QlikView.

Please check **www.PacktPub.com** for information on our titles